MATT AND TOM OLDFIELD

ULTIMATE FOOTBALL HEROES

INIESTA

FROM THE PLAYGROUND
TO THE PITCH

DINO

ISBN: 978 1 78 606 804 0

British Library Cataloguing-in-Publication Data:

A catalogue record for this book is available from the British Library.

Design by www.envydesign.co.uk
Cover illustration by Dan Leydon
Background image: Shutterstock

Printed in Great Britain by CPI Group (UK) Ltd

1 3 5 7 9 10 8 6 4 2

Papers used by John Blake Publishing are natural, recyclable products made from
wood grown in sustainable forests. The manufacturing processes conform to the
environmental regulations of the country of origin.

Every attempt has been made to contact the relevant copyright-holders, but some
were unobtainable. We would be grateful if the appropriate people could contact us.

John Blake Publishing is an imprint of Bonnier Publishing
www.bonnierpublishing.co.uk

For Noah and the future Oldfields to come

Looking forward to reading this book together

Matt Oldfield is an accomplished writer and the editor-in-chief of football review site Of Pitch & Page. Tom Oldfield is a freelance sports writer and the author of biographies on Cristiano Ronaldo, Arsène Wenger and Rafael Nadal.

Cover illustration by Dan Leydon.
To learn more about Dan visit danleydon.com
To purchase his artwork visit etsy.com/shop/footynews
Or just follow him on Twitter @danleydon

TABLE OF CONTENTS

ACKNOWLEDGEMENTS 7

CHAPTER 1 – EL CAPITÁN 9

CHAPTER 2 – THE BAR LUJAN 'STADIUM' 15

CHAPTER 3 – EARNING HIS SHOT 21

CHAPTER 4 – STAR OF THE BRUNETE 28

CHAPTER 5 – LA MASIA 37

CHAPTER 6 – DEBUT DRAMA 46

CHAPTER 7 – THE NIKE CUP 52

CHAPTER 8 – A TASTE OF THE FIRST TEAM 60

CHAPTER 9 – WAITING IN THE WINGS 71

CHAPTER 10 – SUPER SUB 77

CHAPTER 11 – ENTERING THE INTERNATIONAL SCENE 85

CHAPTER 12 – ANNA 93

CHAPTER 13 – EURO STAR 102

CHAPTER 14 – STAMFORD BRIDGE SAVIOUR 109

CHAPTER 15 – KING OF THE WORLD 117

CHAPTER 16 – THE WEMBLEY WIZARD 128

CHAPTER 17 – PENALTY PRESSURE 134

CHAPTER 18 – CHASING MORE TROPHIES 142

CHAPTER 19 – BACK TO HIS BEST 147

CHAPTER 20 – LEADING FROM THE FRONT 152

ACKNOWLEDGEMENTS

First of all, I'd like to thank John Blake Publishing –
and particularly my editor James Hodgkinson – for
giving me the opportunity to work on these books and
for supporting me throughout. Writing stories for the
next generation of football fans is both an honour and
a pleasure.

I wouldn't be doing this if it wasn't for Tom. I owe
him so much and I'm very grateful for his belief in
me as an author. I feel like Robin setting out on a solo
career after a great partnership with Batman. I hope
I do him (Tom, not Batman) justice with these new
books.

Next up, I want to thank my friends for keeping me

sane during long hours in front of the laptop. Pang, Will, Mills, Doug, John, Charlie – the laughs and the cups of coffee are always appreciated.

I've already thanked my brother but I'm also very grateful to the rest of my family, especially Melissa, Noah and of course Mum and Dad. To my parents, I owe my biggest passions: football and books. They're a real inspiration for everything I do.

Finally, I couldn't have done this without Iona's encouragement and understanding during long, work-filled weekends. Much love to you.

CHAPTER 1

EL CAPITÁN

In many ways, it was just like any other game day. Andrés arrived at the Nou Camp three hours before kick-off and, still in his tracksuit, went to look at the pitch. It looked glorious – like an inviting green carpet. The sun was shining and the stands, empty for now, would soon be full of cheering Barcelona fans.

Andrés darted back inside, waving to some of the Nou Camp staff and then stopping to sign autographs for two young boys, one wearing a Lionel Messi shirt, the other with Andrés's own 'INIESTA 8' on the back. He paused for a second outside the Barcelona dressing room, taking in the moment. It was the start of a new season and the start of a new era. 'Here we go,' he said to himself.

He walked in and dropped his bag in the usual spot. He saw that all of his kit was already laid out neatly. No matter how many games he played or how many trophies he won, he never got tired of seeing his name on that famous Barcelona shirt.

Then he spotted the new item, tucked away on a little shelf above his head. The red and yellow captain's armband. It was now his. So many of the leaders who had guided Andrés during his early days in the first team had since moved on, including Xavi, last season's skipper. Now *he* was leading the charge.

'El capitán!' a familiar voice called out.

Andrés turned to see Lionel Messi, whom everyone called Leo, grinning at him from across the room.

'No pressure,' Leo said. 'You just have to lead us to a repeat of last year's Treble-winning season!'

'Thanks, Leo!' Andrés replied, laughing. He was happy to joke about it, but deep down he knew he had big shoes to fill. His teammates would be looking to him more than ever for inspiration. And the expectations were always so high at Barcelona.

Andrés took out his phone and checked his messages. He saw a text message from his good friend Victor Valdés, who he had known since his earliest days at La Masia, the Barcelona academy.

The message read: 'Andrés, today's the day! Your first game as captain of Barcelona. You're going to be great. I still remember the day you arrived at La Masia – what a journey it has been!'

Andrés got kind words everywhere he turned that afternoon as he prepared for the game – a home friendly against Roma. Everyone wanted to talk about the new season and, most of all, his new role.

'Andrés, I remember watching you play when you were this tall,' a Nou Camp worker told him, indicating his own waist. 'And now here you are, leading out the team. I always said you would be captain one day. I just knew it.'

'Don't listen to him,' another worker interrupted, laughing and wagging his finger. 'He says that about every young player who arrives at La Masia.'

'No I don't!'

Andrés smiled. He was beginning to realise that this was an even bigger day than he had thought, but he was ready for the extra responsibility. He had expected the pre-game warm-up to feel the same as it always did. After all, he had been the stand-in captain plenty of times last season. But he quickly saw that this was different. He wasn't just one of the senior players anymore; he had to be the leader and he had to make sure that everyone was focused on doing their jobs.

Even though Andrés had never been a big talker on the pitch, he went to each of his teammates to pump them up and encourage them. He finished by joining Luis Suárez and Javier Mascherano to pass the ball around.

'Don't worry, Andrés,' Luis said, putting an arm on his teammate's shoulder. 'I've got my scoring boots on. We'll make sure you get off to a winning start as captain.'

Andrés smiled. 'That's good because Leo and Neymar were both just telling me that they were going to score more goals than you this season,' he said, with a wink. He was making it up, but he knew it would make Luis play even better.

'Keep it tight at the back,' he said, turning to Javier and sounding serious again. 'Look for me. I'll always be available for a pass.'

Andrés had time for two more stretches and then he jogged back up the tunnel to the dressing room, with his heart thumping faster than usual. It was a hot day and he was already sweating.

Barcelona manager Luis Enrique gave the team his last instructions, keeping it relaxed for the pre-season game. He finished by looking over at Andrés and invited his new captain to add his message for the team.

Andrés smiled shyly. 'Well, you all know how much I love making big speeches,' he joked. His teammates cheered. They were well aware that Andrés preferred to let his feet do the talking. 'Let's carry on where we left off last season,' he said. 'Play like champions. This is the first step towards defending our trophies.'

As he stood in the tunnel with his teammates behind him, the pitch ahead of him and the Barcelona fans singing loudly, Andrés smiled to himself. Even after all the trophies and awards, he sometimes had to pinch himself to believe that he was really living his dream of playing for Barcelona.

He re-positioned the armband one last time and closed his eyes. He took a deep breath and thought about everything it had taken to reach this special moment.

CHAPTER 2

THE BAR LUJAN "STADIUM"

'Come on, we've got time for one more game!' little Andrés called, pulling up his socks. 'Let's make it first to three goals this time.'

'Andrés, I can hardly see you,' replied Abelardo, looking across the park. Like so many of the boys that Andrés played against, he was four years older. 'It's too dark. Aren't you tired of running rings round us all anyway?'

Andrés laughed. His friends were decent players but they fell for his tricks every time. 'Never! I'm not even sweating yet.'

Abelardo shook his head in disbelief – it was easy to forget that Andrés was only six. Yet he was the most natural footballer out of all the boys in Fuentealbilla, their home town. 'Well, we have to go back to the bar to see our parents. Maybe we can sneak into the back room and keep playing.'

The bar was Bar Lujan where Mari, Andrés's mum, worked. It was just around the corner from the park.

'Count me in,' shouted Julian, the third of the three musketeers, 'especially if there's a secret plan involved!' The trio was rarely seen apart.

Andrés grinned. His mum would find out about it eventually, but this idea might just work. They raced off down the street.

'Wait until a few other people go in through the side entrance and then we can walk in behind them,' Andrés explained. 'Stay low to the ground until we get to the curtain. After that, follow me.'

Their timing was perfect. Three men were opening the door just as Andrés, Abelardo and Julian arrived. They scuttled through to the back room and exchanged high fives. 'That was so easy,' Julian whispered excitedly. 'So, what's next? Where are we going to play?'

'Err, and one other thing,' Abelardo added, looking around and smiling. 'We don't have a ball. That's kind of important!'

Andrés laughed. He had forgotten that the ball they were using at the park belonged to one of the other boys.

'They always keep old paper in that corner,' he said, pointing. 'Let's roll up a few sheets into a ball. That'll do for tonight. If we move the table to that side, we'll have space to play.'

Mari was not surprised to hear the sound of footsteps in the back room. She had seen the three boys as soon as they sneaked into the bar. Sensing that they were on some kind of secret mission, she decided to let them have their fun.

'I guess the game at the Bar Lujan Stadium has begun,' she told Abelardo's parents, who were there for dinner that night. 'Thank goodness there isn't anything valuable back there!'

Back in the thick of the action, Andrés was proving

as deadly with a rolled-up paper ball as he was with a leather one. He dummied to run to the right, then knocked the ball to the left. Abelardo was too slow to react and Andrés knocked the ball between the school bag and the jacket, which acted as their temporary goalposts.

'You fool me every time!' Abelardo moaned, picking himself up off the floor. 'I was sure you were going the other way. You're too quick for me to even trip you up!'

'Welcome to the Bar Lujan Stadium,' Julian called, putting on a commentator's voice. 'Andrés Iniesta has just scored his fourth goal of the night. What a special performance to celebrate the opening of the stadium. For young Abelardo, it's a game he may want to forget in a hurry.'

Andrés and Abelardo fell to the floor laughing. 'I love it!' Abelardo said. 'This is such a great back-up place for us to play. It's our own private pitch! We have to keep it a secret.'

But Andrés couldn't resist. That night, Manu, Andrés's cousin, called to tell him that he would be visiting the next weekend. Andrés listened for a few seconds but then cut in to update Manu about the new plans for the bar's back room.

'Manu, you've got to see it. It's perfect for a two-a-side game. Sometimes, if we're not too loud, Mama forgets we're there and we stay up playing way past our bedtime. I'll show you when you get here.'

'Sounds amazing,' Manu replied. 'Keep me a spot for next weekend. Just try not to be too disappointed when I score a hat-trick.'

Andrés laughed. His cousin may have been older and a good player, but Andrés was fearless. 'You'll have to get the ball off me first,' he shot back.

From that summer onward, Bar Lujan hosted many games – sometimes because it was raining, sometimes because it was dark, sometimes because they had lost their proper ball. Whatever the reason, Andrés was always the star.

Whenever Andrés scored yet another goal, Julian high-fived him. The games were always so much more fun for whoever was on Andrés's team. 'For most of us, becoming a professional footballer is a crazy, unlikely dream,' Julian said, putting his arm round his friend. 'But it's not so crazy for you, Andrés. It could really happen.'

CHAPTER 3

EARNING HIS SHOT

Playing against Abelardo and Julian made Andrés feel like a star, but everyone could see that he needed a bigger challenge.

'Andrés, why don't you play for a proper team yet?' Manu asked during one of his weekend visits. 'You're so good but you need to have a coach and go to training sessions. That's the way to really improve.'

Andrés shrugged. 'My dad spoke to a few teams but everyone thinks I'm too small. What do they expect?! I'm only seven. Of course I'm small!'

'Do you want to join me at Albacete? Everyone is really nice there. I can speak to my coach and see if they'll give you a chance.'

Andrés hesitated. He liked the idea of joining Manu's team but feared he might embarrass himself against better players – and he didn't want to embarrass Manu either. 'Erm… yes… but I'd need to check with my dad. Maybe I won't be good enough but I'd like to give it a try.'

'Trust me, Andrés. Once they see what you can do with the ball, they will be begging you to sign.'

Manu worked his magic, telling all the coaches about his little cousin. 'Years from now, you'll be remembered as the coach who discovered Andrés Iniesta,' he told each of them, hoping that would catch their attention.

Later that week, José Antonio, Andrés's dad, got a call from Albacete. He had also been speaking to a few of his contacts there, and asking them to put in a good word for Andrés. 'We've heard some great reviews of Andrés's ability and we'd love to see it for ourselves,' said Ginés Meléndez, the head of the youth system. 'We're holding more trials next Thursday at twelve and we hope to see Andrés there.'

José Antonio didn't need to check the calendar. 'Of course, yes. He'll be there.'

After putting the phone down and jumping around to celebrate, he rushed over to Bar Lujan, knowing that his son would be there with Abelardo and Julian.

'Andrés! Andrés!' he called. 'Great news. Albacete are offering you a trial.'

Andrés had the paper ball at his feet, but he stopped still. 'Really? What... When...?' He had so many questions that he didn't know where to start. He turned to his friends. 'Okay, no dirty tackles before Thursday. I need to be on top form.'

Abelardo and Julian both grinned. 'He thinks he's a superstar already,' Abelardo whispered.

'I'll pick you up from school and we should make it just in time,' José Antonio added. Andrés just nodded and smiled. It was all happening so fast and he had so little time to prepare for it. Maybe that was a good thing.

When Thursday came, it was a desperate rush after school. Andrés gobbled a sandwich on the way, then sat back and tried to stay calm. He knew that Manu had told the coaches to expect big things, and that just added to the stress. Then he wished he hadn't eaten the sandwich so quickly.

José Antonio was driving as fast as he dared, but he still noticed that Andrés looked nervous. 'Just try to enjoy it,' he told his son. 'I think it's great that you're getting this chance but I don't want you to feel any pressure from me or the rest of the family. If this doesn't work out, there are lots of other teams.' He parked the car and they jogged over together to meet the coaches.

Albacete coach Victor Hernandez spotted them and waved them over. 'Hi, Andrés. I'm Victor. I'm one of the coaches for your age group. You're just in time.'

Andrés flashed a quick smile but didn't say anything. José Antonio gave his son a gentle pat on the back. 'Good luck. Show them what you can do.'

He barely had time to warm up before the seven-a-side games began. 'Andrés, join the green team,' Victor called, throwing him a green bib to put on over his T-shirt.

Victor said nothing else, so Andrés introduced himself to the other boys on the green team — two

called Javier, plus Roberto, Paco, Albert and Diego.
'What position do you play?' Diego asked.

'Midfield usually,' Andrés answered, though he
hadn't played enough games to really know what
that meant.

Andrés hoped that the sandwich earlier and a sip of
water would be enough to get him through the trial.
In the end, there was no reason to worry.

He scored two goals in the first few minutes – one
after a dribbling run, the other with a back heel.
Andrés hadn't noticed Victor watching their game but
the Albacete coach suddenly called for him to come
off the pitch to talk to him. Was the trial over already?
Had he done something wrong? Maybe he should
have been passing more to the other boys, he thought.

'Don't look so worried, Andrés,' Victor said,
laughing. 'I only brought you off because I saw
enough in those first few minutes to know that we
want you at Albacete. I didn't want you to get injured
and we need to try out some of the other players. If
we get the forms signed quickly, you might be able to
play next weekend.'

A huge smile broke out on Andrés's face – part relief, part joy. 'Thanks! I'd love to play for Albacete!'

'Great. Let's go over to see your dad and we can work out all the next steps.'

José Antonio could hardly believe what he was seeing. His son had won over the Albacete coaches in less than five minutes. All he had to do now was put his signature in all the right places. Then Victor hurried back to the pitch to watch the rest of the session. Seeing Balo, one of the other coaches, he couldn't wait to share the news.

'We've uncovered a gem today,' he announced, before even saying hello. 'Remember that tiny kid called Andrés? Well, he came for a trial today and he was incredible. He's only seven and has a lot of growing to do, but he has so much potential – his quick feet, his dribbling, his first touch. It's a rare combination in such a young boy.'

Balo joined in the excitement. He knew that Victor was a tough man to please and only used this kind of praise for special cases.

'Is he still out here?' Balo asked, looking round at the two games being played behind him.

'No, I didn't want to waste a single second. His dad has just signed the registration forms. Andrés will be coming back over any minute now so you'll be able to see for yourself.'

Balo saw the same abilities in Andrés that Victor had spotted. The boy was the smallest player on the pitch but he seemed to have the most time on the ball and the most speed. As soon as a defender got close to him, he would just change direction and glide away.

'Wow!' Balo said 'I don't know what else to say. I think that covers it.'

Victor laughed. 'Apart from his height, it's hard to believe he's only seven, isn't it?!'

'I suppose Manu will probably want a fee for his scouting recommendation,' Balo joked.

'Hopefully he'll settle for a thank you, which I will happily give him,' Victor answered. 'It's early days, but Manu might just have delivered a future star to our doorstep.'

CHAPTER 4

STAR OF THE BRUNETE

Before long, Andrés was the star of the Albacete junior teams – his teammates knew it, the coaches knew it and, bit by bit, the league was learning it too. But a bigger test lay ahead.

'Andrés, the Brunete tournament is only a week away,' Manu said, giving his cousin a playful punch. 'Scouts from all the big teams will be there. Don't blow it!'

His sister, Maribel, giggled. 'Yeah! No pressure!'

Andrés didn't need to be reminded. He had the date circled on the little calendar in his room – seven-a-side games against the best teams in the country. He wanted Albacete to do well but the idea of scouts made him nervous – and he had no idea what he would say if one of them wanted to talk to him.

The nerves turned to excitement once he joined his teammates on the bus. The journey to the tournament – being held in Madrid – was slow but there was lots of singing and laughing to pass the time.

The Albacete team were staying at a hotel for the week-long tournament and Andrés was sharing a room with Mario, another of the midfielders. Like Andrés, he loved to talk about football and, well, anything really.

Late that night, as Andrés lay thinking about the next day's big game, Mario still had his lamp on and was reading an old magazine.

'Isn't this amazing?!' he said, getting out of bed to look in some of the cupboards. 'A holiday, a nice hotel with a TV in the room, and no one to tell us when to go to bed. Do you mind if I turn on the TV?'

But if Mario was expecting Andrés to nod and agree, he got a surprise. 'There's no time for that. We need to sleep. We've got a big game tomorrow and we have to be fresh. If we win the first game, you can watch all the TV you want.'

Mario smiled, returned to his bed and reached for the lamp switch. 'Sorry, I didn't realise you were part of the coaching staff now as well!'

After a good night's sleep, Andrés was raring to go. As he got into position in midfield the next afternoon, he blocked out any talk about scouts. But it only took one game for the scouts to notice his quality – how smoothly he controlled the ball, how he never wasted a pass, how effortlessly he found space when there seemed to be none.

'That was a masterclass, little maestro!' Victor said. 'Two goals, two assists and you're just getting started.'

Andrés was exhausted, red-cheeked and guzzling water as fast as he could. He just smiled and nodded.

Watching from further down the touchline, José Antonio was pleased that he had made the trip. He had a huge smile on his face – like a kid in a sweet shop. He knew Andrés was good, very good even, but now he was dominating the Brunete. That meant he was the real deal.

MATT AND TOM OLDFIELD

And Andrés wasn't finished yet. Against all odds, he led Albacete into the final rounds of the Brunete and, since the team had been expected to be knocked out early, it left some of the boys short of clean clothes. Now the mighty Real Madrid stood in their way.

'We're just as good as them!' Andrés suddenly said at the end of Victor's team talk. 'Forget what shirts they're wearing. We have no reason to be afraid.'

Everyone turned around in surprise. Andrés rarely spoke up like that. 'That's just my opinion,' he added quickly with a shy smile.

But his words rubbed off on his teammates. With Andrés controlling the midfield, Albacete stunned their more famous opponents, winning on penalties. Despite losing the final to Racing Santander, it had still been a brave run and a week that Andrés would always remember.

José Antonio beamed with pride as Andrés was named player of the tournament. As he waited to congratulate his son, he watched Andrés talking to Victor. Probably some final words of encouragement, he guessed.

Then he saw three different men come over to speak to them in the space of five minutes. Each time, Andrés shook hands, said a few words and then pointed to his dad.

It had been a long time since José Antonio had played youth football, but he could still spot a scout from miles away. 'Andrés is on their radar,' he muttered to himself.

The first two scouts rushed over to José Antonio and dropped off their cards, inviting Andrés to join their youth team for training. He was going to be a star, they told his dad.

But it was the third scout whose reaction would change their lives. 'Señor Iniesta, I have been a scout for Barcelona for many years. I know a talented young player when I see one. Your son is terrific – he's head and shoulders above most of the boys here.'

'And you think he might be good enough for Barcelona?' José Antonio asked, still a little shocked.

'I do. I'm going to speak to my contacts and, if Andrés is interested, we can set up the arrangements for La Masia. I'm sure you've heard all about our academy.'

José Antonio nodded.

'But I should add that this is a big commitment and we take it very seriously,' the scout continued. 'Andrés would get a room at La Masia, with meals included, throughout his time with the youth teams. You could visit him whenever you want, but I just want to be clear on how the process works. Spots are filling up for next season so we'll need an answer by the end of the month.'

José Antonio paused. The excitement was still whirring through his body, but it was now mixed with some panic. Andrés was only twelve. Could he really cope at La Masia by himself, so far away from his family? But then again, it was Barcelona!

'Okay, I'll speak to Andrés and get back to you. He's going to be thrilled. Thank you again for coming over – it's an honour to have Barcelona interested in Andrés.'

Shaking a little with excitement, José Antonio drove back to the hotel. He called Andrés to his room and shared the news. To his surprise, his son didn't jump around with excitement.

'This tournament was amazing,' said Andrés, 'and it's very cool to have big clubs talking about me. But I just want to focus on Albacete for now. I don't think I'm ready for anything more.'

His dad was torn. He wanted to respect Andrés's decision but he feared that his son was making a mistake. They talked and talked until Andrés had to join his teammates for dinner.

Part of Andrés's prize as player of the tournament was a trip to a theme park. It was near enough to Barcelona that they could stop off to visit and learn more about the club's youth academy.

'Andrés, this is your call,' José Antonio said in the car home that afternoon. 'No pressure from me. You have another week to think it over before we need to let Barcelona know.'

Time passed and Andrés did not bring up the topic again. José Antonio and Mari decided not to mention it in case it put extra pressure on their son. Then, out of the blue, Andrés changed his mind.

'Dad, I've been thinking a lot about the Barcelona offer. I was afraid before, but now I'm more afraid of missing an opportunity to do something I love. Is it too late to go to La Masia?'

José Antonio looked at his son. 'But are you sure this is what you want?'

'I'm sure. I know it's going to be really difficult, but I want to give it a try.'

'Okay, then. Barcelona's deadline has passed but I'll make the call. Let's see what they say.'

Andrés waited nervously in the hallway while José Antonio found the Barcelona scout's business card, dialled the number and explained the situation.

'Yes, that's right... For this year... No... Yes, of course... I see...'

Andrés was trying to make eye contact with his dad. 'What are they saying?' he asked quietly.

At that same moment, José Antonio turned to Andrés with a big grin. He put his thumb up. 'You're in!' he whispered.

Andrés felt a shiver run down his body. He had Barcelona posters on his wall – Pep Guardiola was his biggest hero – and now he would be joining their youth academy.

But he knew that this was just the easy part. Now he had to pack up his clothes and prepare for some painful goodbyes.

CHAPTER 5

LA MASIA

There was silence in the car. Andrés could hear his
heart thumping in his chest as he looked out of the
window. He had been so excited about the opportunity
to train with Barcelona but now, sitting in the back
seat next to his grandfather, with his parents in the
front, he felt scared.

Andrés had no idea exactly how far they were from
La Masia, Barcelona's famous academy, but he sensed
they were close. It would have been natural for him
to be nervous about whether he had the footballing
ability to compete with the other boys at La Masia,
but instead he could only think about the tearful
goodbye that lay ahead.

As the big stone buildings of La Masia finally came into view, Andrés saw his dad shiver. Clearly, this was going to be really hard for everyone.

'We're here, Andrés!' his grandfather announced cheerily, trying to lighten the tense mood in the car. 'This is where the adventure really begins.'

'Aren't you coming in with me?' the boy asked quickly.

'Of course,' José Antonio replied. 'We'll make sure you get settled and meet some of the other boys.'

Andrés took a deep breath and forced a quick smile. 'Okay, let's go.'

José Antonio parked in front of the main entrance and stretched. It had been a long drive. At that same moment, a tall, white-haired man came rushing down the front steps, offering a friendly wave.

'Nice to meet you, sir,' he said, shaking José Antonio's hand. 'I'm Señor Farres, head of the La Masia residence. I hope you had a good journey.'

Andrés appeared at his dad's side, catching Señor Farres by surprise. 'Ah, this must be Andrés. Welcome to La Masia. Follow me. One of the other boys will join us in a few minutes to give Andrés a tour and help him set up his things in the dormitory.'

Andrés nodded shyly and they all shuffled inside. Señor Farres grabbed some paperwork from a table in the hallway.

'As I'm sure you know, many great players have walked the corridors of La Masia. It'll feel like a second home in no time and we'll do everything we can to make you comfortable.' He turned suddenly at the sound of footsteps on the stairs.

'Good timing, Luis!' Señor Farres called. Andrés gulped as he saw the giant figure walking towards him. This boy was almost twice his size.

'Hi Andrés, I'm Luis,' the boy said, holding out a huge hand. 'Ready to look around? Don't worry, I know all the secret places. Just don't tell Señor Farres.' Luis grinned and winked.

Señor Farres smiled. 'I'll pretend I didn't hear that. Have fun. We'll get the registration forms signed and then meet you in the main lounge. Make sure you show Andrés his bunk bed and the drawers for his clothes.'

Andrés's eyes were darting around everywhere, with a mixture of fear and excitement. He still hadn't said a word since getting out of the car – but he didn't know what to say. He was afraid that if he tried to speak, he might start crying.

Before he had a chance to suggest that maybe his parents should come on the tour with him, Luis was guiding him to the stairs. 'I know it feels like a big change at the moment, Andrés, but that will pass. That's the library over there and here's the main cafeteria where you'll have all your meals. There are three bathrooms along that corridor and your dormitory is just ahead on the left. I'll show you which bed is yours.'

Andrés felt the panic building inside him and tears rolled down his cheeks. There were so many thoughts running through his head – he was going to be alone, his family would be hours away, he didn't know anyone.

'This is it,' Luis continued. 'You'll have the bottom bunk. Jorge is in the top bunk and you'll meet him later on. When you unpack your clothes, you can use –'

He could see that Andrés was crying. Not loud sobs, just quiet tears.

'It's okay to be scared,' Luis said, putting an arm on Andrés's shoulder. 'I still remember my first day. It's all such a shock with so many new faces. But it will get better, I promise. Once you get on the training pitch and start kicking a ball around, I'm sure that will help.'

Andrés nodded, wiping the tears on his sleeve. 'Thanks,' he mumbled.

He put on a brave face when they joined his parents in the lounge. His mum hugged him and asked lots of questions about the tour. She offered to help unpack his clothes but Andrés thought the other boys might laugh if they saw her doing that. Instead, they sat and talked. Señor Farres told lots of stories about the future stars that he had mentored at La Masia over the years.

Eventually, José Antonio looked over at Andrés. 'I think it's time we checked in at the hotel,' he said reluctantly. 'We can see you're in good hands here and it'll give you a chance to meet Jorge and the other boys. We'll be back in the morning to drive you over to see the school.'

Andrés hugged both his parents and then his grandfather. He held on tight and could feel the tears building again. But he forced himself to stay strong. He waved and waved until the car was out of sight, then found his way back to his dormitory.

'Hey, Andrés,' a voice called out. Andrés looked around. The light was on but he couldn't see anyone.

'Hello?'

'Up here!' Suddenly a little head appeared from the top bunk. 'I'm Jorge. Nice to meet you. We're going to be bunk mates. Just tell me you don't snore!'

Andrés laughed for the first time that day. 'No, don't worry. You won't even know that I'm here.'

'Great. I've only been here since last week so I'm still getting used to it all, but let me know if you have any questions about how things work.'

'Thanks, Jorge. My parents just left so I'm feeling a bit lost. It's so amazing to be here, with a chance to be part of a club like Barcelona, but I never expected it would be this hard. I'm lonely already.'

MATT AND TOM OLDFIELD

'Well, we'll stick together. You see, you've made a friend on your first day! We'll be in the same class at the same school so you'll probably be sick of seeing me soon!'

Andrés smiled. He was relieved to hear that Jorge was a fellow new arrival who understood how difficult it was to settle in. 'Trust me, a friendly face is just what I need.'

Jorge hadn't learned all the boys' names yet but he did his best to introduce Andrés as they sat down to eat in the cafeteria that night. After such a long day, Andrés could barely remember any of the names.

When they had finished their meal and were putting their trays away, a tall, skinny boy walked over and gave Jorge a playful pat on the head.

'How's it going, pal?' he asked Jorge. 'Anyone giving you any trouble?'

'Hey, no, everything is fine, thanks. Andrés, this is Victor Valdés. He gave me the tour on my first day.'

Victor shook Andrés's hand. 'Welcome, little man! Listen, I'll tell you the same thing I told Jorge. If you need anything, give me a shout. I'm in one of the older age groups so I might not see you out on the pitches, but I'm always around the dorms.' Then he spotted a friend at a nearby table and rushed off.

'He's great,' Jorge said, grinning. 'He's a good guy to have on our side. It seems like people listen to him around here.'

Later, as Andrés lay in his new bed, his thoughts quickly turned to his family. He was sure that they had been holding back the tears too when they said goodbye. Being so far from home was going to be hard for him but he knew that they would be suffering too. He just hoped that they would be able to visit him regularly.

Just up the street, José Antonio and Mari were still awake too.

'Did we do the right thing?' José Antonio asked his wife. 'Our little boy is going to be all alone in a big city and we won't be there to help him. I'm his dad. It's my job to protect him.'

Mari understood her husband's hesitation. 'This is the hardest part, but we've made it this far. Andrés wants to do this and we have to let him try. If he doesn't like it, we'll bring him home. But it has to be his choice.'

José Antonio nodded. 'I know you're right. My feelings are just so muddled. I'm terrified for Andrés but at the same time I want him to succeed at Barcelona. It's going to break my heart when we drive home tomorrow, but I get little goosebumps whenever I imagine him wearing that famous Barcelona shirt. I guess we'll just have to wait and see.'

When Andrés finally drifted off to sleep, he had that same dream-like image floating through his head – running out at the Nou Camp as part of the Barcelona first team. It all felt so far away, but he was in the right place to turn that dream into a reality.

CHAPTER 6

DEBUT DRAMA

Andrés's alarm clock buzzed and he reached out
sleepily to turn it off. Half opening his eyes, he
checked the time.

'What?! No!'

He jumped up and turned on the light. All the other
bunks were empty. It was 8.40 am and his first game
for the Barcelona Under-13s team was a 9 am kick-off.
He must have set the wrong time for his alarm. There
was no time to eat or shower. He just threw on his
clothes, picked up his boot bag and rushed out of the
room. 'I can't believe this,' he muttered as he leapt
down the stairs, two at a time.

Luckily, the pitch was just round the corner. He

could see his teammates finishing their warm-up as he sprinted across the grass.

'I'm so sorry!' he panted. 'I messed up my alarm, but I'm here now.'

He paused to catch his breath.

'We were starting to worry,' said Eduardo, one of his coaches. 'No problem. Just put that Number 5 shirt on. You're starting in the centre of midfield. By the looks of it, they're a tall team so let's keep the ball on the deck and move them around. Long balls aren't going to work today.'

Andrés nodded. He changed quickly and ran over to join one of the small passing circles.

'Why didn't you wake me before you left?!' he asked Jorge, still more embarrassed than angry. 'I almost fainted when I saw the time!'

'Sorry, Andrés. I took my bag to breakfast and then went straight to the pitch. I thought you'd be a few minutes behind me.'

Andrés was still doing a few stretches as the game started. It was so unlike him to be this unprepared, but he was soon up to his usual tricks. He stepped away to find space and cushioned the ball effortlessly. He allowed his marker to get close before gliding past him, then a quick body swerve left another defender on the ground. As other defenders backed off, Andrés dribbled on and then played the perfect through ball. Jordi, the team's main striker, didn't even need to take a touch before firing the ball into the bottom corner. 1-0.

'You'd never know that he has just rolled out of bed,' Eduardo whispered to the other coaches. 'Or that this is his first game. He's got it all.'

Two minutes later, Andrés controlled a high pass on his chest and, without hesitation, curled a shot into the top corner. The goalkeeper didn't even move. Even the referee looked stunned.

'Imagine what he could do if he had breakfast,' Jorge joked at half-time. Everyone laughed, even Andrés, who had hoped people would quickly forget about how late he was.

Andrés completed his hat-trick early in the second half with a tap-in and then scored a fourth after a one-two with Jorge.

'Let someone else have a chance!' Jorge said with a big smile. 'You're a man on a mission today! Set me up for one, or are you still blaming me for arriving late?'

Andrés grinned. 'I'll try.'

At one point late in the second half, three defenders surrounded Andrés near the corner flag and closed in looking for a bit of revenge. But Andrés weaved past one, knocked the ball through the legs of another and then laid it off to a teammate before the third could crunch him. He could do nothing wrong that morning.

He felt dizzy as he joined Jorge and the other boys for lunch. His stomach was growling.

'How do you make it look so easy?' asked Juan, one of the team's defenders, as they put fruit and bottles of water on their trays.

'I love to wait for the defender to make the first move. As soon as they're off balance, I can beat them with one quick move – a drop of the shoulder, a change of pace, a stepover.'

'Well, you went through the whole set of moves

today! It was almost cruel what you did to those defenders. I'm glad I don't have to mark you.'

'I just can't believe I almost missed the game. I was two seconds away from silencing the alarm and falling asleep again. No debut, no goals.' He shivered at the thought.

'You've set a pretty high standard for yourself now,' Juan added. 'How do you follow up four goals on your debut?'

But Andrés wasn't worried. Even though he was still missing his family, he found a sense of calm whenever he had the ball at his feet. And he was starting to feel at home at La Masia. He and Jorge had their routine and their hiding places for sweets and chocolates that their families sent. Despite all the training and matches, they still kept up to speed with their schoolwork too.

Meanwhile, the Barcelona coaches had quickly spotted Andrés's potential and were quietly making plans for him to play for the older age groups. 'We've got to keep pushing his limits and test him against the best,' was a regular comment among the coaches.

Andrés still had doubts about whether he would ever be good enough to get all the way to the first team, but he was starting to realise that he had a very special gift.

CHAPTER 7

THE NIKE CUP

As the Andrés fan club continued to grow, so did the boy's abilities. The more time he spent with his La Masia family, the stronger the connection became on the pitch. They knew each other's styles of play inside out and had the kind of confidence that comes from rarely losing. Now in the Under-15s team, Andrés and his teammates had already won most of their games by half-time.

'We're unstoppable,' Jorge boasted after their third 6-0 win of the season. 'It's about time someone gave us a real game.'

'Well, careful what you wish for,' replied Serra Ferrer, one of the leaders of the Barcelona academy, as he headed out of the changing room. 'We're playing in the Nike Cup this season against the best teams from around the world. There will be no easy wins against them.'

'Bring it on!' Jorge replied, high-fiving Andrés. 'We'll be ready.'

Ferrer suddenly reappeared in the doorway. 'Oh, I forgot to mention the best part. If you reach the final, you'll get to play at the Nou Camp.'

That grabbed everyone's attention. There was silence in the room. Andrés began daydreaming about what that would be like – running around that perfect pitch, taking the same steps that his heroes took for every home game, and waving to his parents and sister in the crowd. 'Could there be any better motivation for us?' he said to Jorge as they walked back to the team minibus.

Two months later, he no longer needed to dream about that experience. With a few scares along the way, Barcelona were in the final and Andrés would be playing at the Nou Camp.

'I have to keep checking the noticeboard to make

sure it's not some kind of cruel joke,' he told Victor when they saw each other in the cafeteria. 'This is going to be so special.'

'We'll all be there cheering for you,' Victor replied, ruffling Andrés's hair.

Even though he had been at La Masia for a few years, Andrés had rarely set foot inside the Nou Camp. One of his few visits had been as a ballboy for a league game – an experience that placed him just yards from the first team stars.

But this time he would actually be on the pitch. He would be changing in the dressing room and walking down the tunnel. Every time he thought about it, his whole body tingled with excitement.

'We don't get to play at the Nou Camp every week but this is still our home,' Ferrer said on game day, giving his final instructions to a room that was a mix of energy and nerves. 'No one comes into this stadium and pushes a Barcelona team around.'

It was no secret that, in the Barcelona team, Andrés was the man to stop – and so it was no surprise that Rosario, their opponents from Argentina, sent two or three defenders to swarm around him whenever he got the ball. In the first half, that plan worked. Andrés had no time to make things happen and twice he fell to the ground because of bruising tackles.

'Andrés, we need you further forward to unlock this defence,' Ferrer said at half-time. 'I know you like to drop deeper to start the move but we want you just behind the strikers. We'll get the ball to you. That team is really well organised so we need to be more direct.'

It made a difference instantly. The Rosario defenders and midfielders were pointing and arguing about who should mark Andrés as he roamed free. Soon it was 1-1. Andrés whipped in a free kick and Jordi headed the ball in.

'Let's go again,' Andrés yelled as they ran back to the centre circle. 'Let's win this.'

Barcelona were in control and Andrés kept making runs into the box. Sometimes the defenders made desperate clearances, other times the pass was too high or too long. But then in the final minute Jorge gave him the perfect chance. Andrés burst through and poked a well-placed shot past the diving goalkeeper.

Gooooooooooooooooooaaaaaaaaaaaaaaaaaaalllllllllllllll lllllllllll!!!!!!

As he turned and ran back towards his teammates, he suddenly realised what he had done. He had just scored a last-minute winner at the Nou Camp.

Determined to help the defenders, Andrés dropped back. Rosario were thumping long balls straight into the box and, while Andrés wasn't likely to win many headers, he could fight for the knockdowns. One clearing header bounced towards him and, for once, he didn't even look up to play a pass. He just kicked the ball as hard as he could down the pitch towards the corner flag.

When the final whistle sounded, Andrés fell to his knees and put his arms in the air. 'We did it!' Jorge yelled, pulling Andrés up and hugging him. Their teammates rushed over to join the celebrations. 'Champions at the Nou Camp!' Andrés shouted, with a huge smile all over his face.

They shook hands with the Rosario players and

wandered over towards the touchline, thinking that Ferrer would want to give a quick team talk. A few of the players sat down on the edge of the pitch. 'Wait a minute,' Ferrer called, rushing over. 'You can rest later. This is your moment. Your fans are waiting for you.'

Andrés was confused. He turned to Jorge who had a similar puzzled look on his face. 'What?'

'Your victory lap. Come on, you're at the Nou Camp! Walk round and clap the fans.' He smiled. 'You've got to savour every moment when you win a trophy!'

Andrés led the way, jogging down the touchline and waving to the fans, who were still cheering even five minutes after the game had finished. 'The stadium isn't even half full and it's still so loud,' Jorge called. They spotted friends and family in the crowd and blew kisses.

'This is a day we'll never forget, no matter what happens in our careers,' Andrés said. 'I'm glad I'm sharing it with you, Jorge.'

'Oh stop it – you're going to make me cry!' Jorge joked.

Then it was time for the trophy presentation. 'Ladies and gentleman,' a tournament organiser announced, holding a microphone and waving for silence. 'What a great tournament and a thrilling final. Congratulations to both teams. Now for the trophy – I'd like to invite the Barcelona boys to come up.'

With his socks rolled down to his ankles, Andrés followed his teammates onto the little stage for a team photo. 'Since the final was played here at the Nou Camp, we've got a Barcelona player to present the trophy,' the organiser added. 'Please welcome Pep Guardiola!'

Andrés was speechless. He just stared as Pep appeared from behind a group of men to the left of the stage. Was this really happening? All of Andrés's teammates knew that Pep was his favourite player.

'Andrés has a poster of Guardiola on his wall at home,' José Antonio told one of the other parents, partly to explain why his son looked so shocked.

'Great game today and such a calm goal at the end,' Pep told Andrés as they posed for more photos.

'I'm pretty sure that won't be your last goal in this stadium.'

As Pep walked away to chat with other players and parents, Andrés – still short for his age – felt ten feet tall. Since arriving at La Masia, he had always hoped that he would become a professional footballer, but there were often some doubts. Now that Pep thought he could do it, he believed more than ever that he would one day play for the Barcelona first team.

CHAPTER 8

A TASTE OF THE FIRST TEAM

Andrés knew he was getting closer and closer to the first team. He heard the whispers around the club and the praise from his coaches. He had even seen a few scouts and first team staff on the touchline at his games lately.

Jorge always had a theory that people were watching and usually decided that any adult he didn't recognise was probably there to report back on Andrés's performance. 'You'll be moving up soon. I can feel it.'

But Andrés still took nothing for granted, working harder than ever in training. Even after being called up to the Spanish Under-16s squad and winning the

Under-16s European Championships, he kept his feet on the ground. 'We'll see' was his answer whenever anyone suggested that he'd soon be promoted. After all, there were so many good players at Barcelona.

However, he soon saw that Jorge was right. The next week, Andrés was substituted in the second half with the team winning 4-0. He had set up all four goals. He looked at Ferrer in surprise. 'Me?' he checked. The coach nodded and signalled for him to jog over.

'Don't worry, Andrés,' he explained, sensing the youngster's disappointment. 'I just want to keep you fresh. I'm going to be in trouble if I send you up with an injury.'

He stopped speaking and grinned, letting the words hang in the air. It took Andrés a few seconds to catch up.

'Wait, what? The first team?'

Ferrer laughed. 'Of course, if you don't want to join the first team practices, I can always tell them no,' he teased.

'No, no! I mean, yes! I want to join the practices.

You just surprised me, that's all. Wow, this is such an honour.'

'You've earned it, Andrés. Most people think it's just about talent here – the fastest player, the most skilful player or whatever. But we look at much more than that. Teamwork, character, personality – that all matters too. You're ready. We all agree.'

Andrés watched the last ten minutes of the game in silence. His head was spinning. His teammates were racing around and even scored a fifth goal, but he barely noticed. His legs suddenly felt very heavy. He was going to be sharing a pitch with his idols – and that was great and scary at the same time.

When the big day arrived, Andrés practised his handshake in front of the mirror to make sure he wouldn't look silly. He arrived early for training but suddenly realised he didn't know which entrance to use. After ten minutes wandering around the outside of the building, he started to panic.

At that moment, a car honked its horn and slowed down to a stop next to him. The window rolled down ...d Andrés froze.

It was Luis Enrique, another player that Andrés
loved to watch.

'You're Andrés, right? We've all heard a lot about
you and I recognise you from the Nike Cup final.
I was there that night. Jump in and I'll show you
around.'

Andrés took a second to steady himself. Was he
really talking to a Barcelona player? Not just that, a
player who recognised him?!

'Great, thanks. I was afraid that security wouldn't
believe that I was here to train with the first team. I
probably look like a young fan to them!'

Luis Enrique laughed. 'I guess I was just in time
then.' He parked the car and jumped out. 'Ready to
meet the rest of the team?'

Andrés nodded, but inside his stomach was already
doing back flips. What was he going to say when he
came face-to-face with more of his heroes?

They walked into the cafeteria and Andrés's eyes
darted from side to side. There were star players
everywhere – Rivaldo, Frank de Boer, Patrick Kluivert,
Marc Overmars, Phillip Cocu.

'Lads, I want to introduce Andrés. He's going to be training with us.'

Andrés shuffled round the room and shook hands. He loved meeting the players but he was glad that part was over. He was also relieved to see Xavi, who he had met a few times at La Masia.

He got directions down to the dressing room and wandered over to a spot in the far corner where his training kit was laid out.

His nerves disappeared once he had the ball at his feet. While they waited for the coaches, Andrés joined in with one of the rondos. He quickly saw how effortless it was for the others – a little flick here, a quick touch there to keep the ball away from the players chasing in the middle. But he did well, even saving one bad pass from Rivaldo with a flick of his own.

When the other coaches arrived, they got into pairs to run through some drills. Andrés felt a hand on his shoulder. 'I'm with the young gun.' He turned to see Pep Guardiola standing next to him. Andrés's mouth dropped open but he quickly recovered to shake Pep's hand. 'I had a feeling I'd be seeing you again soon,' Pep said.

Andrés watched Pep closely, trying to learn from him. They moved from heading and passing to shooting and free kicks. Pep made everything look easy, but Andrés was still pleased with his own effort. He was proving that he belonged there.

'The club is predicting big things for you,' Pep said as they took a break for water. 'Keep working hard and you'll be a big part of Barcelona's future.'

Month by month, Andrés could see his game improving and by the time Louis van Gaal took over as manager, Andrés was already knocking on the door for first team minutes. One afternoon after training, Louis spotted that Andrés was still out on the pitch doing some shooting practice. Andrés whipped the ball into the top corner just as his manager walked over.

'Andrés, I was going to tell you this tomorrow but there's no reason to wait,' Luis said. 'You've been doing great work in training and we want to reward that.'

Andrés felt a little excitement building in his chest.

'You get better every session,' Louis continued. 'So now it's time to push you even further. You're going to be starting in midfield against Bruges in midweek.'

Andrés tried not to smile too much but it was too late. 'That's amazing. Thanks, boss.'

'Just play your game,' Louis added. 'Don't overthink things. We've already qualified for the next round, so this is a chance for us to see some of you youngsters in action.'

Andrés could barely eat or sleep – and apparently his parents were just as nervous as he was. He was very quiet on the flight to Belgium, even though there were other La Masia boys in the squad with him. He just counted down the hours to kick-off.

He froze when he walked into the dressing room and saw the 'INIESTA 34' shirt hanging in the far corner. In all the thoughts that had crossed his mind in the build-up to the game, for some reason he hadn't pictured his name on the back of the shirt.

Out on the pitch, he tried to relax. His mind was racing but after a simple pass with his first touch, he felt better. Later in the first half, he picked up the ball about thirty yards out. His first thought was to slide a pass behind the defence, but when he dribbled forward, the Bruges defenders backed off. 'Why not?' Andres thought. He glanced up and swept a curling shot high towards the goal. He watched as the ball curved in slow motion and thumped against the bar. So close!

'Great effort,' shouted Carles Puyol, another La Masia boy in the first team that night.

Barcelona eventually got their goal – from Juan Román Riquelme, another player whom Andrés admired – and Andrés's first team career was off to a winning start.

'What a feeling!' he said to Carles as they walked back to the dressing room. Seeing Carles and Victor, good friends from La Masia, make it into the first team had given Andrés extra motivation to join them.

'You had a great game, Andrés,' Carles replied, slapping him on the back. 'You nearly had a debut goal as well!'

Louis had more good news for Andrés later that

season. 'The Barcelona fans are desperate to see you
out there, and I'm going to give them what they
want,' he said, smiling. 'We're playing Recreativo at
the weekend and you'll be starting just behind Patrick.
We need a spark and you're the guy to give us that.'

Andrés had been nervous before the Bruges game,
but this was even more nerve-wracking. This was the
Nou Camp, in front of over 100,000 fans. 'I've got to
make a good first impression,' he told Jorge and Victor
the day before the game. 'I need the fans on my side.'

'The more you worry about the fans, the more
likely it is that you'll flop,' Victor said. Jorge gave him
a harsh look but he continued. 'I'm just being honest.
Take it all in and enjoy the atmosphere, but then focus
on playing your game. Louis wouldn't have picked
you if he thought you couldn't handle the moment.'

Andrés felt better already. 'You're right. I can do
this.'

The waiting in the tunnel seemed to go on forever.
He stretched his neck from side to side and jumped
up and down, trying to shake off the nerves. Finally,
there was movement at the front of the line and

Andrés walked out to the biggest cheers he had ever heard.

'All the hard work, all the training sessions, all the sacrifices have led to this moment,' Louis had told him as they left the dressing room, giving him a pat on the chest. 'Enjoy it.'

Within minutes, Andrés's nerves had gone. He wanted the ball and took every chance to dribble at defenders. By half-time, the Nou Camp had a new hero. Andrés laid the ball off for Simão to score the first goal, then a dazzling one-two with Patrick should have led to a second but Patrick thumped a simple chance over the bar. He and Andrés both stood with their hands on their heads.

Andrés had more magic up his sleeve for the second half, darting between defenders and always looking for Patrick's runs. Barcelona won 3-0 and Andrés had been the star man.

'Get over here!' Louis said loudly, hugging Andrés. 'What a performance! That's one of the best games I've ever seen a youngster play on this kind of big stage. Congratulations!'

Andrés's phone buzzed non-stop for the next hour, with friends and family celebrating his big night. 'I didn't want the game to end,' he told his dad that night. 'I would have played all night.'

José Antonio laughed. 'Well, you'd better save some of that energy! You've convinced Louis and you've won over the fans. You've got lots more games ahead.'

CHAPTER 9

WAITING IN THE WINGS

Andrés had shone in every age group at La Masia and he had been an instant hit in the first team. But his smooth road was about to get bumpy. When Louis was replaced as manager, Andrés had to press the reset button and win over his replacement, Radomir Antić.

But that was to be an uphill battle, as more experienced players moved up the pecking order and new signings made it tougher for Andrés to prove his worth.

He just didn't know where he stood – was he making the kind of progress that the club expected? Did they have a plan for giving him more opportunities? He had a lot of questions and no one seemed to have the answers.

Time and again, he was left on the bench – and sometimes he wasn't in the squad at all.

'I need to be playing,' he told his parents. 'I'm doing everything they tell me, but I'm not getting a chance. A few months ago, I was playing in the big games. Now they're giving those minutes to other players.'

'Your chance will come,' his dad José Antonio said reassuringly. 'I truly believe that – maybe there will be an injury or a suspension. But we can speak to the club on our next visit. Then you'll have more information.'

Andrés's friends could also tell that the situation was making him tense. 'If this continues, would you consider leaving Barcelona to get more experience?' Abelardo asked that summer.

'No way.' The words were out of Andrés's mouth before he had really thought about the question. He just couldn't picture himself playing for any other team, even on loan. 'This is Barcelona. I can be patient and I'm confident that I'll get my chance eventually. It just hasn't worked out yet.' As he repeated his dad's message, he hoped that he was right.

'I just don't understand why they're spending money on all these players when the future of their midfield is right under their noses,' Abelardo continued. 'It seems like such a waste.'

But Andrés refused to sulk. Instead, he worked even harder in training and kept a smile on his face. Antić lasted only six months as Barcelona's manager, with Frank Rijkaard taking over as his successor. Frank was promising a new era at Barcelona and he made it clear that Andrés would feature in his plans. That didn't happen at first, but eventually he got some playing time off the bench.

'You might not feel it yet, but this whole experience is making you tougher – adjusting to La Masia, climbing the ranks and fighting for a place in the team,' Mari said when Andrés provided an update. 'Mentally, you're strong enough to handle anything.'

'I'm sure you're right. As long as I'm getting some

game time, I can catch the eye – even if it's as a sub for now.'

That quickly became his role, giving him lots of opportunities to get on the scoresheet as defences tired. But he remained desperate to play from the start of a game, just as he had done when Louis was in charge. Having had that taste of the spotlight, it was difficult to be happy with a reserve role.

Still, there were plenty of moments that made him smile, like his first goal for Barcelona against Levante in the Spanish Cup. Striker Javier Saviola did most of the hard work but Andrés was in the right place at the right time. 'I'm with you!' he yelled as he sprinted forward. Saviola dribbled round the goalkeeper but his shot was deflected and it just trickled towards the empty goal.

Andrés pounced on the loose ball and fired it into the net, just as two defenders slid in at his feet.

Goooooooooooooooooaaaaaaaaaaaaaaaaaaalllllllllllllll llllllllllll!!!!!!

Ronaldinho and Saviola raced over to celebrate, putting their arms round Andrés.

'You have to buy us all drinks,' Ronaldinho said, smiling. 'That's the rule when you score your first goal!'

'You little poacher!' Saviola added, laughing. 'You snatched that goal from me!'

Andrés joined in the laughter. 'It wouldn't have crossed the line and you know it!'

It was one of the easiest goals he had ever scored, but one that he would never forget. He still couldn't believe he was sharing the pitch with Ronaldinho, probably the best player in the world at the time.

'It feels good to be involved but I want to prove I can play ninety minutes every game,' he told José Antonio later that month. 'It's so much more difficult to get into the flow of the game as a substitute and I think I can really help the team in a bigger role.'

Another part of the problem was that people looked at Andrés and compared him with Xavi, often deciding that there was only room for one of them. 'I'll play anywhere,' Andrés told Abelardo. 'They all think Xavi and I are too similar but I know we can work well together.'

He sighed. It was definitely frustrating but he had come too far to worry about it. As the 2005/06 season began, he hoped that his luck was about to change.

CHAPTER 10

SUPER SUB

Frank Rijkaard gathered the Barcelona team together in the training ground meeting room. Andrés sat nervously as his manager waited for the last few players to sit down before reading out the starting line-up for the following week's Champions League final against Arsenal.

Andrés looked across his row and saw Ronaldinho sharing a joke with Samuel Eto'o. They were both going to be starting – they had no reason to worry. But for others, like Andrés, it was not so easy. He had been in and out of the team during the season, though he had been a key man in the previous round. He felt he deserved to play alongside Xavi in midfield, though he feared that Frank might have other ideas.

'Listen up, guys. Wednesday night is a huge game. It's more than just a Champions League final; it's our chance to show Europe that Barcelona are back.'

The players cheered – Andrés more quietly than most. He was still wondering if he would have a chance to play a part in it all.

'Okay,' Frank continued, 'I want to name the team now so that those who are starting are well prepared. We're going to need the full squad to win this final so we'll be relying on our substitutes to give us a lift with energy.

'At the back, Valdés, Olegeur, Puyol, Márquez, van Bronckhorst.'

No surprises there, Andrés thought. His stomach was doing somersaults. Just get it over with, he thought.

'In midfield, Edmilson, Deco, van Bommel.'

Andrés's heart dropped. He just stared at the floor, refusing to let his disappointment show. He felt a few eyes turn in his direction but still didn't look up. He didn't even hear the rest of the line-up. A single fact was spinning round and round in his head: I'm not starting in the Champions League final.

When the meeting was over, Andrés stood up slowly and walked towards the door. He just wanted to get home as fast as he could, before he let his feelings show.

Just as he was picking up his bag, Victor appeared with a sympathetic look on his face. 'Andrés, I know you're hurting at the moment, but we're going to need you on Wednesday. I guarantee it. I'm not sure why you aren't starting, but make sure you're ready. It's okay to be angry today but clear your head for Wednesday.'

Andrés nodded. It was good advice.

That afternoon, he called his dad. 'Dad, I got some bad news today. I'm not starting in the final.'

José Antonio's first thought was a flash of anger. How dare they not start Andrés?! But he knew being angry wouldn't do Andrés any good. 'I'm sorry, son. I know how hard you've worked. I think it's a mistake, but there's nothing you can do about it now. Even though you're not starting, it doesn't mean that you won't have a chance to help the team.'

Andrés paused, picturing himself coming on as a substitute and scoring the winner. 'I suppose so,' he finally replied. 'If it's a close game, hopefully I can make the difference.'

He refused to feel sorry for himself. Barcelona were in the Champions League final and Andrés wanted to support his teammates in any way possible. Still, as he boarded the plane, he could feel the excitement of those who were in the starting line-up. As they had dinner at the hotel in Paris, he saw the focus on their faces as their minds began to picture the big game ahead. The disappointment burned in Andrés's chest.

The next night, he warmed up with all of his teammates, as usual. He passed the ball back and forth with Carles, looking around the stadium as it began to fill up. Despite wishing that he was playing, there was only one thing he cared about: Barcelona lifting the trophy.

But a roller-coaster first half left Andrés biting his nails nervously on the bench. First, he was jumping up as Arsenal goalkeeper Jens Lehmann fouled Ludovic Giuly and was sent off. 'With an extra man, we just need to keep moving the ball around,' he whispered to Henrik Larsson on the bench. 'Arsenal will be exhausted.'

That plan was dented when Arsenal stunned the whole stadium by taking the lead. Andrés couldn't believe it. He put his hands over his face but quickly removed them in case anyone thought he was sulking. Andrés could see that Frank was angry with how the team was playing.

When the half-time whistle blew, the Arsenal fans roared; the Barcelona fans were noticeably quiet.

Andrés walked slowly towards the tunnel. 'We've still got forty-five minutes to turn this around,' he said to himself.

Suddenly, Frank appeared next to him. 'Andrés, you're going on for the second half.'

Andrés's heart skipped a beat. He hadn't expected to be brought on so soon. 'Okay, great,' he finally replied.

'We need to get control of the flow in midfield and just calm things down. You're the man for the job. Use the half-time break to warm up on the pitch and then we'll run through the final instructions.'

Andrés grabbed a ball from one of the Barcelona assistants and jogged back up the tunnel to the pitch. He only had fifteen minutes to loosen his body and sharpen his mind. He went through his routine of stretches again and got comfortable with the Paris pitch.

As his teammates reappeared for the second half, Andrés saw Frank waving for him to join him on the touchline. He was holding a thin folder and wanted to give Andrés more details on his role.

Andrés did his best to listen, but he just wanted to get the game going again.

The Barcelona fans cheered loudly as Andrés's arrival was confirmed on the loudspeaker. He quickly got into the action, winning a tackle in midfield and firing a pass out to Ronaldinho on the wing. As Andrés had predicted, the more Barcelona knocked the ball from side to side, the more Arsenal looked tired.

'We've got to make it count,' he said quietly to

Samuel Eto'o as they waited for a throw-in. 'We're
running out of time!'

Moments later, a slick pass and a neat lay-off set
up Eto'o, who drilled the ball home. 1-1. Game on.
Andrés raced over to celebrate. As they got back
into position for the kick-off, he looked up at the big
stadium scoreboard. There were still thirteen minutes
to go – and he felt like the freshest player on the pitch.

He kept dropping deep to receive short passes from
Carles and Rafael Márquez, then launching quick
attacks. Finally, Arsenal were undone again. Henrik,
also fresh off the bench, created an opportunity,
which was finished off by Juliano Belletti, another
of the subs, who bundled in a low shot through the
goalkeeper's legs. The comeback was complete!

Then it was time to celebrate. Andrés shook hands
with the shocked Arsenal players. Thierry Henry
walked over and patted him on the shoulder. 'You
picked us apart when you came on,' Thierry said.
'That changed the game.'

Carles and Victor raced over to hug Andrés and
then they joined the rest of their teammates leaping

around in the centre circle. This was the Champions League final experience that Andrés had been craving – and one that he had feared he would miss out on as a substitute. The final had not started the way that Andrés had hoped, but the ending was everything he had dreamed of.

CHAPTER 11

ENTERING THE INTERNATIONAL SCENE

Andrés had played his part in Barcelona's success in Paris but he knew there were areas of his game that he needed to work on. That was all part of the process. He was still only twenty-two but his reputation was growing fast. He was so focused on the Champions League final and his ongoing development, he hadn't even thought about the World Cup that summer.

'So... the World Cup – what do you think?' Abelardo asked him during a visit to Barcelona.

'It's going to be a great tournament,' Andrés answered. 'There are so many good teams. I'm probably going to spend some time with my parents over the summer so let's make plans to watch a few games together while I'm back.'

Abelardo laughed. 'Sometimes you're too modest for your own good! I was asking about whether you thought you'd make the Spain squad. You might be *at* the tournament, Andrés!'

Andrés dismissed the idea immediately with a wave of his hand. 'Come on, I haven't even played a game for Spain yet! Give me another two years, then I'll have a shot.'

'Well, sometimes they take younger players to give them some experience ready for future tournaments. Who's a bigger future star than you?'

'I think you're a bit biased! Trust me, we'll have plenty of time to watch the matches together.'

Still, it made Andrés think. Maybe there was a small chance that he would be picked. He should at least keep an eye on the TV, he decided.

On the morning that the squad was due to be announced, Andrés's phone buzzed at 8 am. It was too early for his parents to be calling and he had spoken to his sister the night before. He picked up his phone and didn't recognise the number.

'Hello?'

'Hi Andrés, this is Luis Aragonés.' Andrés froze. The Spain manager. 'I'll keep it short. You'll see the news later this morning but I wanted to personally let you know that you have been selected for the World Cup squad. Congratulations.'

He was speechless. Was this really happening? The World Cup?

'Andrés, are you still there?'

'Sorry, yes. This is unbelievable news and I'm still taking it in. Thank you for telling me. It's an incredible honour.'

'We'll be back in touch with all the details later today. I'm looking forward to working with you in Germany.'

When the call ended, Andrés had to sit down. His hands and legs were shaking. Then he rushed into the lounge to turn on the TV, slipping on the floor on the way and almost crashing into the door.

He grabbed his phone again and called his parents.

Mari answered. 'Mum, I'm in the World Cup squad!
They picked me!'

He heard Mari shouting the news through the
house. José Antonio was there in seconds, panting
from rushing down the stairs.

'Oh my goodness!' Mari said. 'What a dream! I
can't believe my little boy is going to the World Cup!'

'I'm on my way to get a Spain shirt with Iniesta
on the back!' José Antonio added, laughing.
'Congratulations, son. That's wonderful news! A few
of the newspapers said you might have a chance but I
didn't want to jinx it by believing it.'

'Even if I just carry the drinks, this is going to be
amazing,' Andrés said.

'We're so proud of you!' Mari said. 'I know you'll
be putting pressure on yourself to do your best, but
make sure you take the time to enjoy it as well.'

Andrés smiled. His mum knew him too well. He
was already thinking about how many chances he
might get to play and how he could make a good
impression.

He had always dreamed of playing in the World

Cup but he was realistic about his own role in the squad. There were many talented midfielders for Luis Aragonés to choose from – and they were all more experienced and established than he was. Andrés was determined to learn as much as he could from them.

But it was quickly clear that he would be doing more than just watching from the bench. Luis gave him his debut in a pre-tournament friendly and Andrés played well, proving that he was not afraid of the bright lights of international football. It felt almost magical to pull on the famous red Spain shirt and he couldn't help but stand in front of the mirror in the dressing room – just to make sure it was all real!

As he sat at the first squad meeting, he looked around at his teammates and was struck by the same feeling as when he had started training with the Barcelona first team: there were so many stars! Raúl and Michel Salgado sat in the row in front. Xabi Alonso was in the row behind.

Andrés wasn't sure where to sit so he just found an empty seat. He was relieved when his teammate Xavi sat down next to him. At least there were plenty of Barcelona players in the squad.

'Let the World Cup adventure begin!' Xavi said, grinning. 'Ready to take on the best in the world?'

'Bring it on!' Andrés replied.

Spain made a strong start to the 2006 tournament, winning their first two games. Andrés remained on the bench but joined in the celebrations. The day before the final group game, Luis called him into a meeting room after training.

'Andrés, you'll be starting against Saudi Arabia. We want to shuffle things up a little. We've been really impressed with everything you've done in training. Just bring the same approach tomorrow – find space, look for the killer pass, and take on defenders.'

Andrés couldn't stop smiling. He was just nodding and nodding. 'Thanks. I won't let you down.'

As soon as he was back in his hotel room, he dived onto the bed and jumped up and down. He grabbed the phone and called his parents.

'Dad, I'm in the team for tomorrow's game! I'm going to be starting a World Cup game! I just found out so don't tell too many people. I'm not sure how I'm going to sleep tonight!'

José Antonio bit his lip to hold back proud tears. 'That's fantastic, son!' he managed to reply after a long pause. 'We'll all be watching. Your uncles and cousins are already planning to come to watch the game at our house so I'll try to keep it a secret for as long as I can. We were just talking about trying to spot you among the substitutes so they'll get a bit of a surprise when you're right there on the screen!'

It took Andrés a while to fall asleep but eventually he managed to relax. 'It's just another game,' he told himself.

As he walked out onto the pitch, he saw large sections of red in the crowd. He had stood in the line for the national anthem plenty of times before, but it had never made the hairs on his neck and arms stand on end in the way it did that afternoon.

Once the game started, he made the most of his opportunity. With the La Masia message fixed in his mind – receive, pass, offer, receive, pass, offer – he was involved in every attack.

Spain won the game 1-0 and kept up the momentum for the next round.

'I've got a 100 per cent winning record!' Andrés said, laughing. 'What a game. I know everyone has already moved on to thinking about the second round, but I'll never forget today.'

Unfortunately, only a few days later, he was packing his bag. After all the positive signs in the group stage, Spain flopped in the knockout round, losing 3-1 to France. As he had expected, Andrés was left on the bench and it was a very quiet dressing room after the game, followed by a silent drive back to the hotel.

For some of the squad, the 2006 World Cup would be their last one. Andrés could tell that was extra painful for them, but he had learned a lot – both about how he could succeed on the international stage and about Spain's shaky track record at big tournaments. 'There's so much talent but we just can't get it right,' he told his parents. 'If I get more chances, I'm going to change all that.'

CHAPTER 12

ANNA

'Come on, Andrés!' pleaded Nino, a friend he had made since moving to Barcelona. 'Don't be so boring. You'll enjoy it. You're focused on football all the time – this will give you a break. This party is going to be huge.'

Andrés sighed. He wasn't a big fan of parties and bars, but Nino was the third person that week who had encouraged him to take his mind off football and have some fun. Maybe they were right.

'Okay, you win. I'll come for a few hours but I'm not staying late.'

Nino grinned. 'I'll settle for that.'

They were at the party for less than thirty minutes.

It was a disaster. No one showed up and the air conditioning was broken.

'This is the last time I let you plan things,' Andrés whispered to Nino, who looked even more miserable than he did.

But Nino had at least succeeded in getting Andrés to take a night off and he was not ready to give up just yet. He had an idea.

'Let's go to El Teatro,' he said, grabbing Andrés by the arm. 'It's just round the corner and they always have live music.'

Andrés shrugged. It had to be better than the party. 'Okay, I'll come for a little while,' he replied.

But all Andrés's indifference changed immediately when they walked into El Teatro. He saw a girl standing behind the bar.

'Okay, Nino. I take it all back!'

The place was still quiet. Nino led the way to the bar.

'Hi, I'm Nino. This is Andrés.' Andrés gave his usual shy smile.

'I'm Anna,' the woman replied, giving a little wave.

'Andrés is having a rare night off. So let's have your most exotic cocktail.'

'No, no,' Andrés interrupted. 'Ignore him. I'd be falling over after two sips. We'll just have two orange juices please.'

'Coming right up,' Anna laughed.

A skinny man with a big beard sat down a little further along the bar. He glanced at Andrés and Nino, then looked back, staring for longer.

'You're Iniesta!'

Andrés went red. He always found these moments awkward.

He nodded, hoping that the man would settle for being right. But he quickly saw that was unlikely.

'I'm Francisco – pleasure to meet you. Can you sign my T-shirt?'

By now, a few more heads were looking up from their drinks. Anna was back with the juices and watching with interest.

As much as Andrés wished he could just run out of the door, manners were important to him. He shook hands with Francisco, took a pen from Nino and neatly wrote his autograph.

'Good luck for the rest of the season! Barcelona are always better when you're on the pitch.'

'Thanks.'

Anna smiled. 'Shame on me for not realising we had a famous person in the room tonight,' she said, making fun of Andrés. 'Can we show you to our VIP area?'

Andrés laughed. 'Now that you mention it, I was wondering why there was no red carpet laid out on the street.'

'It's not too late,' Anna replied, giggling. 'We can arrange something. Would a rug work?'

Andrés looked to his right and saw that Nino was chatting with Francisco.

'Honestly, it's nice to talk to someone about something other than football.'

'You've picked the right person then,' said Anna. 'My whole family are Barcelona fans – and they're going to be very jealous when I tell them I met you – but I've never understood all the fuss.'

Andrés smiled. 'Honestly, I prefer it that way,'

he said. 'All the attention feels kind of weird. I love playing football but it's a job, like any other.'

'Well, you were very nice with that guy. I'm sure you've made his night.'

And meeting you has made my night, Andrés thought to himself. He was pleased to see that the bar was still half-empty so Anna could stay and talk.

'So, let's pretend I'm a big fan. How is the season going?'

'Pretty well so far. It's still early days but we think we can win some trophies again this season. And we've got this young star called Lionel Messi who is going to be the best player in the world in no time.'

Anna was nodding. 'I've heard of him.'

'Of course,' Andrés replied, rolling his eyes and pretending to be sad. 'Everyone loves Leo. You've just never heard of me!'

They both laughed.

'It was really nice to meet you, Andrés. I don't usually work here but a friend asked me to help out tonight – I'm glad I said yes.'

The crowds were piling into El Teatro now. Anna

gave him an apologetic smile and went to serve other customers. Every now and again, she would glance over at Andrés.

A while later, Andrés was yawning. He had no chance of talking to Anna again with so many people queuing at the bar.

'Let's get going while it's still easy to find a taxi,' Andrés said to Nino eventually. It was hot in the pub and he was starting to sweat.

'Spoilsport!' Nino said, grinning, as they left and walked to the taxi queue. 'At least admit you had a good time.'

'You're going to use this as an excuse to drag me out more often, aren't you?' he replied.

Nino laughed.

'It was fun,' Andrés admitted, as he climbed into the taxi. But then his shoulders slumped. 'I just wish I had been brave enough to ask for Anna's phone number. I was going to but then I chickened out. Maybe she would have said no anyway. Then the bar got busy and the chance was gone.'

Nino sat and listened, then a little smile broke out on his face.

'You think it's funny?!' Andrés asked, pretending to kick Nino in the shins.

'Watch it! No, no. Actually, I was just thinking that I might be able to help with that. I think Anna is Jordi's friend so maybe it's not too late.'

Andrés was suddenly hopeful again. 'Okay, yes, text him. Ask him for Anna's number. Please!'

Nino laughed. 'Are you the same guy who didn't even want to leave the house tonight?'

'Fine. I'll say it. You were right. You know best. I'll always remember to listen you from now on. Just please get me the phone number.'

'Wow, you really like her!'

Andrés shrugged. 'I'd like to get to know her better. I'll admit that.'

He sent text after text to Jordi and finally got Anna's number. He prepared a message, then re-wrote it five times. Would she even remember who he was?

Andrés pressed 'Send' and waited. A few hours later, his phone buzzed with a new message from

Anna. 'Ah, the big Barcelona star. Of course
I remember! Dinner sounds great. Where and
when?'

They went out for dinner one week, then lunch
and two dinners the next week. Conversation was
easy and for Andrés it made such a nice change to talk
to someone who was not focused on Barcelona. He
picked smaller restaurants and was relieved that no
one seemed to recognise him.

After a few months, he decided it was time to plan
a bigger surprise. He scribbled a note on a scrap of
paper and left it for Anna: 'Pack a suitcase.'

Later that afternoon, he got a call from Anna.
'Andrés, what's going on? What's this big plan?'

'It's a secret. If I tell you, I'll ruin it.' He
laughed. 'I'll pick you up at five o'clock. No more
questions.'

Andrés rarely took breaks during the Barcelona
season but they had a few days off and he wanted
to make the most of it. They went to a nearby town
with restaurants by the water and endless fields for
walking.

He was as peaceful as he could ever remember feeling, and he already sensed that Anna was going to be a part of his life for many years to come.

CHAPTER 13

EURO STAR

'What a difference two years make!' Maribel said as she and Andrés had coffee at his house. 'At the World Cup, you were on the bench and gaining experience. Now you'll be in the starting line-up.'

Andrés smiled at his sister. 'I'm hoping you're right.' He had learned so much from being part of the World Cup squad, but this time – in the 2008 Euro championship – he wanted to be in the thick of the action.

'Just promise you'll still remember your sister when you're on the victory parade with the trophy!'

But Andrés just shook his head and held up his

hand. 'Hang on, one step at a time. We've got a lot of work to do first.'

A week later, manager Luis Aragonés repeated that same message to Andrés and the rest of the Spain squad as they prepared for their first group game against Russia.

'The hard work starts now,' he said. 'This team has so much potential but I don't need to remind you about 2006 or other big tournaments in the past. We've had talented teams before, then fallen flat on our faces. Same old Spain, that's what everyone says.'

He paused. 'Look around the room. Go on. Look.'

Andrés hesitated but then turned to see Xavi on his left, then Fernando Torres on his right. He and Fernando had played together in the Spain youth teams.

'Never forget that we're all in this together,' Luis added. 'You guys have the chance to change the story this summer by bringing home the trophy. If we play our game and keep our heads, we can beat anyone.'

When Luis revealed his starting line-up, Andrés wanted to punch the air in excitement. He was in!

'I've got a good feeling about this tournament,'

Andrés told Fernando as they warmed up. 'I've looked at all the other teams and there's no one we should be afraid of.'

'Are you trying to put a jinx on us now too?' Fernando said, firing the ball at Andrés.

'Oh come on. Do you really believe in that nonsense? We just haven't played well enough in the past, but this can be our moment!'

They made a flying start, with Andrés leading the charge. David Villa scored early in the game to settle the nerves, and Andrés joined Xavi in keeping the ball away from the Russians with quick passing.

Just before half-time, Andrés drifted in from the wing and dribbled forward. With one glance, he saw David's run and guided the ball through. David made no mistake. 2-0.

Andrés had set up goals in big games before, but this one was extra special. He jumped on David's back as they celebrated by the corner flag.

'Wow, listen to the fans!' David shouted. 'You'd think this was a home game. It's so loud.'

By the final whistle Spain had defeated Russia 4-1.

Spain kept the momentum going in their next two
games, winning the group and sneaking past Italy on
penalties in their quarter-final. Andrés was getting
comfortable in his role. In most games, he came off
with thirty minutes to go as Luis turned to another of
the midfield playmakers, but he was happy with his
performances.

'It makes sense for the manager to use fresh legs in
the second half,' he told his dad on the phone after
the quarter-final. 'I just want to make sure I'm playing
well enough to keep my place as a starter.'

'You're doing that, Andrés,' José Antonio reassured
him. 'You're always involved in the build-up play and
you've linked well with Fernando and David. Keep
your head up. There's a big moment ahead for you – I
know it!'

Spain may have defeated Russia in the tournament's
first game, but the Russians had done well enough in
the group stage to qualify too, and so the teams met
again to compete for a place in the final.

'Don't look too far ahead,' manager Luis warned.
'The minute you start thinking about playing in the

final, the dream will slip away. And forget about that
first game of the tournament against Russia – that
scoreline means nothing now. They will be better
this time.'

But Luis was wrong. Spain remained as dominant
as in the opening group game. Andrés played an even
bigger role this time. It was his cross that finally gave
Spain the lead. He cut inside from the left wing, spotted
Xavi racing into the box and fizzed in a low cross. Xavi
just steered the ball into the net. That goal settled the
nerves and set Spain on the way to a 3-0 win.

'We're within touching distance now!' Andrés
told Anna on the phone that night. 'After all the
disappointments at big tournaments, we have the
chance to give the fans a proper party.'

As they prepared for the final against Germany, Luis
appeared suddenly and put his arms round Andrés
and Xavi. 'If you guys control the tempo, we'll be just
fine. We play to our strengths. We might not have the
biggest strikers or the trickiest wingers, but we have
the midfield passers. It's hard for opponents to hurt us
when they don't have the ball.'

Andrés did his best to stay calm. He looked around
the stadium while the captains met in the centre circle
for the coin toss – and he saw lots of red shirts.

That was all extra motivation – and Andrés
responded with his best game of the tournament. He
almost set up a goal in the first half, drilling in a low
cross and putting his hands over his face as the ball
was deflected just wide.

But later in the first half, Fernando broke free and
put Spain ahead. Andrés raised both arms and let out
a loud scream.

Andrés was playing so well that Luis did not make
the usual substitution at the sixty-minute mark. As
Spain clung to their 1-0 lead, he made another burst
forward into shooting range. He fired in a quick shot
but the ball was cleared off the line by a desperate slide.
Again, Andrés was left holding his head. So close!

In the end, one goal was enough. The referee blew
the final whistle and Andrés jumped into the air,
waving his arms. They had done it!

'Can you believe this?' he yelled as Victor rushed
over to hug him. 'What a night!'

'Campeones Olé!' they all sang, linking arms.

'The best part is that we're still a young team,' Andrés said with a huge smile, one arm on Xavi, the other on Fernando. 'This is just the beginning for us. Watch out world!'

Just when Andrés thought the summer couldn't get any better, his phone buzzed. He was on holiday with Anna and enjoying the break.

'Hey Andrés – have you heard the news?' Abelardo asked.

'No, my phone has been off. What's happened?'

'Nothing bad. Don't worry. I just wanted to let you know that Pep Guardiola has been announced as the new Barcelona manager.'

A big smile broke out on Andrés's face. His hero was now his boss. 'This is going to be so much fun!'

As he walked back out to the beach to join Anna, Andrés whistled a happy tune. Even after such a busy summer, he could hardly wait for pre-season training to begin. Little did he know that a roller-coaster season lay ahead.

CHAPTER 14

STAMFORD BRIDGE SAVIOUR

'I think I'm just going to move into the physio's room permanently,' Andrés said, with a big sigh. 'I spend more time there than I do at home.' The 2008/09 season had been cruel to him, with injuries to both legs forcing him to watch from the bench, just at a time when he wanted to help Pep settle into the manager's job.

Anna looked up from her book and gave him a sad smile. 'I'm glad you're trying to joke about it. But I wouldn't blame you if you wanted to scream. You've been so unlucky.'

He shrugged. 'It's just so hard to see the other players arriving for training or matches, while I'm getting treatment all the time. I want to be out there helping them.'

Every time Andrés felt he was getting back to his old form, a new injury would leave him crushed and angry. His teammates did their best to keep his spirits up and Pep was always there to give him support.

'Just keep working hard on your recovery,' Pep told him one morning as they stood together on the training ground touchline. 'We need you back out there but you have to take your time. It's the big games in April and May when we'll need you the most.'

Andrés nodded but deep down it was getting harder and harder to stay positive.

Still, he gave every ounce of effort to his recovery. He owed it to himself and his teammates to fight to get back on the pitch. And, when it came to those big games that Pep had talked about, Andrés was ready to make up for lost time.

'It feels so good to be back,' he told Leo as he heard the Barcelona fans singing his name before the team's El Clásico game against Real Madrid.

'Who are you again?' Leo teased. 'You look familiar but I can't remember your name.'

'Not funny!' Andrés snapped back, followed by a little grin. 'I haven't been away that long!' He threw one of the warm-up cones at Leo.

It didn't take long for Andrés to hit top form. He ripped Real to shreds with his passing and movement, setting up a 6-2 thrashing.

'What a special night,' he told Xavi, putting his arm round his midfield partner. 'Now we just need to do it all again against Chelsea on Wednesday.'

Barcelona were only ninety minutes away from the Champions League final. But Chelsea had other ideas in this second leg of their semi-final. For Andrés and his teammates, it was one setback after another. Michael Essien scored a screamer, Éric Abidal was sent off and they were creating nothing up front. A 1-0 scoreline would be enough for Chelsea to reach the final. 'We've got to wake up,' Andrés said to Leo at half-time. 'This is terrible!'

Andrés kept glancing at the scoreboard as the clock ticked on. 'We just need one chance,' he muttered under his breath. With just two minutes to go, Barcelona had not managed a single shot on target and a heartbreaking semi-final exit was looming. The dream of winning the Treble was hanging by a thread.

Still, while there was time, there was hope. Dani Alves burst clear down the right and Andrés raced forward to support the attack. While others sprinted into the penalty area, he waited patiently on the edge of the box as Chelsea half-cleared and Leo picked up the loose ball. Three defenders rushed to stop Leo from shooting and Andrés saw his chance. 'Leo, square it!' he yelled over the noise of the panicking Chelsea fans.

The rest happened in slow motion. Leo spotted Andrés out of the corner of his eye, and rolled across the perfect pass. As he stepped towards the ball, Andrés knew this was their last chance. 'No time for anything fancy – just smash it,' his brain told him in that split second. He could sense Chelsea defenders charging out towards him, ready to throw their bodies in the way.

But he didn't rush it. He let the ball come across

his body and fired it with the outside of his right boot. The shot arrowed past the diving defenders and into the top corner. Stamford Bridge fell silent.

Goooooooooooooooooaaaaaaaaaaaaaaaaaalllllllllllllll llllllllllll!!!!!!

The joy of the moment took over. 'Yes! Yes! Yes! Get in!' Andrés pulled off his shirt and raced over to the corner flag, throwing himself on the turf. His teammates followed, screaming and screaming. Victor sprinted the length of the pitch to join in. 'You little genius!' he shouted when Andrés finally emerged from the bottom of the pile. 'Andrés, do you realise what you've done? That's one of the biggest goals in Barcelona history!'

Andrés dragged himself back up the pitch for the restart. Every muscle in his body ached, but he didn't care. Pep was dancing up and down the touchline. Back in Spain, José Antonio was in dreamland. His son had saved the day and people all over town were celebrating.

At the final whistle, the Chelsea players ran furiously towards the referee, complaining about earlier decisions. But Andrés didn't see any of that. He was buried in more hugs. He jumped up and down in the centre circle with Carles, Victor and Xavi. 'We're going to the final! We're going to the final!' they sang loudly.

Back in the dressing room, it all began to sink in for Andrés. What a goal! He was so used to seeing Leo or Eto'o score the spectacular goals. This time, it was his turn.

Suddenly Carles and Victor lifted Andrés into the air and the other players rushed over to help. 'Andrés! Andrés! Andrés!'

But, in a season of so many ups and downs for Andrés, there was a fresh blow just around the corner. In the next game, against Villarreal, he felt another pain in his leg. 'Oh come on, no way!' he yelled as he limped off the pitch. The Champions League final against Manchester United – and a chance to complete an amazing Treble – was less than a week away. 'How bad is it?' he kept asking Emili, the Barcelona physio. 'I can't miss the final! I just can't.'

He stopped off to see the massage therapist when

he got back to the hotel. 'Have you missed me?' he asked smiling. 'Whatever it takes, I'll do it. Just get me back on the pitch for the final.'

Ramón, the club doctor, checked in on Andrés all week. They assessed his progress and recommended more treatment. With just two days until the final, the verdict was in. 'Here's the good news – we think you're fit enough to give it a try in the final, as long as you make some adjustments,' Ramón explained. 'Andrés, this is going to sound silly but I mean it: whatever you do, don't shoot.'

Andrés frowned. 'What?'

'We've done our best but your kicking muscle is very weak and very fragile. You can run, you can pass, but shooting will be the problem.'

'Okay, I can do that.'

Driven by the memories of sitting on the bench for the first half of the 2006 Champions League final, he found a way to overcome the pain. And he was determined not to just limp his way through the game. Early on, he picked up the ball in midfield and saw he had space to run. As a Manchester United player finally got close to him, he slid a pass through to Eto'o on the right hand side of the box. Andrés hovered on the edge of the box for an outlet pass but Eto'o squeezed past two defenders and fired a low shot into the net.

'Wooooo!'

'Andres, that was all you!' Eto'o replied as they celebrated by the corner flag. 'Your run and pass made it happen.'

With Andrés at the heart of everything, Barcelona beat Manchester United 2-0 to clinch the Champions League trophy.

'We did it!' he shouted, hugging Carles and Xavi. 'We won the Treble!' As the rush of the final began to wear off, he noticed the screaming pain in his thigh more and more.

Still, he hobbled up for the trophy presentation. As he kissed the trophy and lifted it high in the air, it was hard for Andrés to believe that things could get any better. But a year later, even after another injury-wrecked season, he proved himself wrong.

CHAPTER 15

KING OF
THE WORLD

Andrés had been in the Spain squad long enough to
know all about previous World Cup disappointments.
'Ready to add a World Cup winners' medal to your
trophy room?' he asked Gerard Piqué as the team
boarded the plane for South Africa in the summer of
2010. 'Euro 2008 was special but imagine the feeling
of lifting the World Cup!'

'If you work your magic, Andrés, we can do it!'
Gerard answered.

Andrés went quiet. Deep down, he feared that his
injury jinx might prevent him from doing anything
magical on the pitch. It had been a familiar story over

the previous few years, with one injury after another leaving him on the treatment table.

He had paid a heavy price for playing against Manchester United in Rome a year earlier. He had torn his thigh so badly that it took months to undo the damage – though he had no regrets. After missing so many games for his recovery, the World Cup was the light at the end of the tunnel.

'Switzerland, Chile and Honduras – that's not an easy group, but we've got so much talent in this squad,' Gerard continued.

'We've got a target on our backs now as European Champions, though,' Andrés noted. 'Everyone is saying that we're one of the favourites. There's more pressure than ever.'

'Andrés, the higher the pressure, the better you play! Don't worry!'

Spain manager Vicente Del Bosque, who had taken over from Luis Aragonés in 2008, pulled Andrés aside before training and asked the question that everyone wanted to ask. 'How is your leg?'

Andrés was so thankful that Vicente had named

him in the World Cup squad despite the injury doubts.
He wanted to be positive but he knew Vicente needed
an honest answer. 'It's still sore. But I'll get more
treatment once we're at the hotel. I'll be ready to go
for the first game. I guarantee it.'

Vicente smiled. He looked relieved. 'That's great
news. See how the treatment goes and we'll talk again
tomorrow.' Vicente knew that even a half-fit Andrés
was a dangerous weapon, but he was worried about
using him too soon.

Andrés felt good heading into the first game of the
group, against Switzerland – but things changed late
in the second half. A crunching tackle late in the game
sent him flying to the floor, and he felt a shooting pain.
'No! No! No!' he yelled, slapping the turf.

He limped off and went straight back to the
dressing room with the physio. Oscar, one of the team
doctors, joined them.

'It's not so bad, Andrés. Nothing is torn or broken.
You just need to rest it.'

The pain in his leg was made worse by the final
score. 1-0 to Switzerland.

'I've got to be back for the next game,' he told Anna on the phone that night. 'If we lose again, we could be knocked out.'

The doctors did their assessments and met with Andrés to give the verdict.

'Andrés, I know you don't want to hear this, but you need to rest,' Oscar explained. 'Don't push it for the Honduras game or your tournament might be over. We'll get you ready for Chile instead. We just need more time.'

Andrés tried to argue but he knew Oscar was right. Everyone was working so hard to help him get fit – how could he be angry? He had no confidence in his leg at the moment and he might just make things worse by trying to play. 'Okay, you're right. A few more days could make a big difference. But I want to keep up all the treatments – all day and all night if necessary.'

Oscar grinned. He knew Andrés was serious. 'You say the word and I'll be there. Trust me, you'll thank me when you're playing in the final!'

Andrés smiled. He hoped he was right.

By the time of the Chile game, Andrés was able to take part in a full training session and felt a lot sharper. 'I'm ready,' he told Vicente.

Vicente crossed his fingers. Spain had beaten Honduras but still needed a result against Chile. 'Okay, business as usual!'

Andrés felt a little rusty in the first few minutes. Vicente and Oscar got his attention during a break in play and started gesturing. Thumbs up or thumbs down. 'I'm fine!' he called, giving the thumbs up.

He played better in the second half. David Villa had already given Spain the lead, and then it was time for Andrés to step up. He was stronger in a 50-50 tackle with a Chilean defender before passing the ball in-field and running into the box. David pulled the ball back and Andrés saw it all in slow motion. Instead of swinging wildly at the ball, he just angled a low shot into the bottom corner. He watched the goalkeeper's arm stretch out but it was too late. The ball nestled in the net. Andrés rushed over to celebrate with David.

Gooooooooooooooooooaaaaaaaaaaaaaaaaaaaallllllllllllll llllllllllll!!!!!!

'We needed that goal!' David said. 'It gives us a bit of breathing space now.'

And that came in handy. Chile pulled a goal back, but Spain hung on for the win.

'Well, the group stage didn't exactly go to plan, but we made it through,' Andrés said to Xavi once they were back in the dressing room. 'That's all that counts.'

And Spain did just enough in the next two rounds as well – two 1-0 wins. In the quarter-final against Paraguay, Andrés made a game-changing run, bursting forward from midfield to tee up Pedro. David tapped the ball in when Pedro's shot hit the post.

'How did you have the energy to outrun their whole midfield?' David asked, hugging Andrés.

Andrés just winked.

The same game plan worked in the semi-final against Germany – another 1-0 win. This time, Carles was the hero with a header from a Xavi corner.

'I can't let you attackers have all the fun!' he called as they jogged back into position.

There were less than twenty minutes to go and Andrés couldn't relax yet. He just pushed himself

MATT AND TOM OLDFIELD

to chase every ball. 'Slow it down,' he yelled as one
of the defenders thumped the ball down the pitch
desperately.

Finally, the referee reached for his whistle. Spain
were in the final!

They all ran to Carles, ruffling his already-scruffy
hair. 'Get in!' Andrés screamed, hugging every
teammate. The Netherlands were Spain's opponents in
the final – and Andrés could hardly wait three days for
it. Even better, Anna had booked a flight to be there
for the big game.

This is it, he thought when the day eventually
arrived. He made his way down for the team's
breakfast meeting at the hotel and tried to stay loose.

'Okay, here we are again – another big final!'
Vicente said. 'Embrace the moment, follow the game
plan and we'll be bringing the World Cup home with
us. Wow, that sounds pretty good, right?'

Andrés joined in as they all cheered.

As he went through his final preparations, he had
a sudden thought. Maybe it was the emotion of the
final. He needed a vest and a pen. He rushed over to

123

the kit man and explained his plan, then he ran out for the warm-up.

'Ready to be a hero?' asked Sergio Busquets, who they all called Busqi. 'It doesn't get any bigger than this.'

Andrés nodded. 'We're ninety minutes away from lifting that trophy. We can't let it slip through our fingers.'

But Spain struggled against a well-organised and physical Dutch opposition. Andrés was shoved and tripped. Xabi got kicked in the chest. There were plenty of yellow cards but no one was sent off. 'Come on, ref. What do they have to do to get a red card today?' complained Busqi.

'Just leave it, Busqi,' Andrés called, rushing over. 'We'll just win it the hard way.'

As extra-time ticked away and a penalty shootout approached, Andrés put his hands behind his head and tried to catch his breath. By now, all the players were exhausted. With five minutes to go, Andrés forced his aching legs to run. The game was end to end, with tired tackles everywhere.

Spain launched a quick attack down the right wing
and the ball came inside to Andrés, who back-heeled
it to Cesc Fàbregas to keep the move going. But he
didn't just stand and watch. Fernando had the ball on
the left wing, leaving no one in the box. Why not?
Andrés thought. He sprinted forward just in time for
Fernando's cross. The ball was half-cleared but Cesc
poked it forward and suddenly Andrés was half a yard
in front of his marker.

With every muscle in his body screaming at him,
Andrés took one touch and the ball sat up perfectly
for a half volley. Just like at Stamford Bridge, he knew
there was no time to think about what to do next. He
just put his head down and hit the ball as hard as he
could towards the bottom corner.

Andrés looked up to see his shot power past the
goalkeeper's hand. The net rippled and the world
around him stopped. His mind froze. He didn't know
where to run.

*Goooooooooooooooooaaaaaaaaaaaaaaaaaalllllllllllllll
lllllllllll!!!!!!*

Suddenly, his brain clicked back on. The vest. He

ran to the corner flag and threw off the shirt to reveal the message on his vest: 'Dani Jarque, always with us', in memory of one of his best friends in football, who had died the year before. Dani had been the captain of Espanyol, and despite the rivalry between them and Barcelona, the two had always gotten along brilliantly off the pitch. It meant everything to Andrés to be able to dedicate this moment to his great friend.

He barely had time to straighten the vest to show the message before his teammates piled on top of him. It had to be the winner.

Carles grabbed Andrés in a big bear hug. 'Andrés, your right foot just won the World Cup!' he shouted.

The seconds ticked down and the final whistle finally came. Andrés fell to his knees and his teammates raced over, burying him in hugs again. In the crowd, Anna was crying tears of joy.

Andrés had seen the World Cup trophy on TV many times. Seeing it up close, it was shinier and more beautiful than ever. He lifted it high in the air, thinking of his friends and family – and Dani, of course. He could feel tears of joy bursting to get out.

MATT AND TOM OLDFIELD

And that was just the start of the celebrations. The players returned to Spain to be greeted with a huge parade, just as Maribel had predicted. There were people packing the pavements on every street, with red shirts and red scarves everywhere.

People often asked if he got tired of winning trophies. Was it less special since he had a room full of them already? 'Never,' he always replied. 'I never want it to end!'

CHAPTER 16

THE WEMBLEY WIZARD

After winning the 2010 World Cup that summer and the Treble the year before, there was a danger that things might seem too easy. But, back at Barcelona, Pep quickly brought everyone back down to earth.

'Where are our World Cup winners?'

Andrés and Victor were the first to step forward.

'You guys probably need some extra running after all the champagne you drank in South Africa,' Pep said, chuckling. 'Grab all the training cones for a start!'

Pep smiled as the rest of the squad cheered.

'So much for us being heroes on our return!' Victor joked as they scooped up the cones.

The following week, Pep entered the cafeteria just as Andrés was leaving.

'Andrés, hang on a second. I want to talk to you.'

Andrés sat down, wondering why his manager sounded so serious.

'Do you remember the impact it had on you when you joined the first team and saw how hard the senior players work? I need you and Xavi and the other senior players to keep setting the right tone. The younger players and the new signings look up to you. We can't get sloppy. We can't start believing we're unbeatable. At the moment, we just don't seem focused enough in training.'

Andrés nodded. 'We'll clean that up. Don't worry. Sometimes I forget how long I've been here – long enough to speak up, I guess.'

Pep smiled. 'Don't worry. I'm not asking you to suddenly be the guy who screams and shouts. I just want you to know how valuable you are to this team and how much influence you have.'

Andrés sat in silence for a moment. He definitely wanted to be someone the youngsters could look up to. 'Thanks, boss. Actually, this is good timing as I'm going to have to set the example at home soon too.'

Pep looked at him, with a puzzled expression.

'I just found out that I'm going to be a dad in April.'

Pep leapt up from his seat to give him a big hug. 'Oh wow, such great news. Good luck with those early mornings!'

Even as he focused on the season ahead, Andrés would never forget his big World Cup final moment – and there were plenty of people around ready to remind him.

As they warmed up for an early season away game, the stadium announcer was reading out the teams. 'For Barcelona, Valdés.' 'Boooo!' 'Alves.' 'Boooo!' And on it went.

'Iniesta.' There were no boos. Instead, most of the home fans jumped to their feet and started clapping.

Andrés was usually too involved in his own warm-up to listen to the line-ups, but even *he* noticed the cheers. 'Oh come on,' Leo called from across their passing circle, laughing. 'Now they love you here as well? Who doesn't love Andrés?!'

'After that goal, I think you're welcome in any stadium in the country!' Xavi said.

As Andrés jogged over to the touchline for a final drink of water, the fans nearby again stood to applaud. He waved back.

'I'm still getting used to all these nice away fans,' he joked with a few of the substitutes standing next to him.

The league season was up and down, but nonetheless Barcelona marched towards the Champions League final.

For Andrés, it was another chance to finally play a full, injury-free Champions League final, again against Manchester United. 'Third time lucky,' Anna said, hugging him before he left for the airport. Andrés gave her a kiss and then tiptoed into the nursery to kiss his little daughter, Valeria.

'Make sure Mummy watches the game, okay?' he whispered.

In 2006, he had been watching from the bench in the first half. In the 2009 final, he had been in so much pain that it was hard to fully enjoy the experience. This time, 2011, he felt great. He took in every little detail – the banners in the crowd at Wembley, the Champions League anthem, the special stitching on his shirt.

But once the game started, he was in his special zone. In the first half, it was Andrés's clever pass that released Xavi, who set up Pedro for the first goal. They raced over to the Barcelona fans. Most of the crowd at Wembley was supporting Manchester United, but this corner of the stadium was all purple and blue.

United equalised, but Barcelona pulled away in the second half. Leo and David both scored beautiful goals, with Andrés pulling the strings in midfield.

As the United players chased and chased, Andrés was always available for a quick pass. Then he slipped away and found more space. United were just chasing shadows. He could see how angry they were getting.

'They're really tired,' Xavi said. 'Let's keep moving the ball around.'

'Just look out for some crunching tackles,' Andrés replied.

As the seconds ticked away, Andrés could feel the

excitement building. They had followed the game plan perfectly and now they were to be champions of Europe again.

'We've got our trophy! We've got our trophy back!' they sang as the party went late into the night. Andrés loved every minute of it, but by the time he was back home, he was already thinking about the next trophy he could set his sights on.

CHAPTER 17

PENALTY PRESSURE

Andrés sat down on the pitch, grabbed a water bottle and looked around at his teammates. 'We couldn't have done much more,' he said quietly to Fernando. 'It just wasn't our day.'

Extra time was over and their Euro 2012 semi-final against Portugal would have to be settled on penalties.

'But we still have a chance,' Fernando replied. 'Fancy taking one?'

Fernando was joking. He knew Andrés was not a penalty taker – and never had been.

It took Andrés a couple of seconds to reply. 'Yes, I want one.'

Fernando looked up with eyebrows raised. 'What?

Are you serious? Andrés, you hardly ever even practise them!'

But it was too late to talk him out of it. Andrés got to his feet slowly and walked over to Vicente. 'Boss, let me take one of the penalties.'

Vicente looked about as shocked as Fernando had. 'Andrés, are you sure?'

Andrés just nodded.

'Okay,' Vicente said, scribbling on a sheet of paper to update the order of penalty takers. 'You'll have the second one. Good luck!'

Andrés joined his teammates as they walked to the centre circle, lined up and linked arms. Their hearts were pounding. He could feel the nerves running through his body but also a sense of pride. He was one of the senior players in this squad, he had won every trophy on offer and he wanted the responsibility of coming through in a big moment for his country.

There was silence among the players as Xabi's penalty was well saved, then jumping and clapping as Portugal also missed their first penalty. Now it was Andrés' turn.

He took a deep breath and walked towards the penalty area. The walk took forever. He didn't want to rush. He needed to stay as calm as possible. He scooped up the ball and placed it carefully on the spot. Then he marked out his run-up and blocked everything out – the consequences of missing, the crowd noise, the goalkeeper moving around on his line. He just waited for the whistle.

When it came, Andrés took one last glance at the goal, without giving any clues about which side he would be aiming for. He ran forward and fired the ball hard towards the bottom right corner. A half-second later, he looked up to see the goalkeeper diving to the other side, and the ball hitting the back of the net.

'Get in!' he yelled, pumping his fist and pointing to the Spanish fans. He was so fired up. He jogged back to the centre circle to watch the rest of the action.

'Great penalty,' Fernando told him, hugging him and leaving his arm on his shoulder. 'When was the last time you took one in a game?'

'About ten years ago, I think. Maybe more!'

Fernando laughed. 'Only you, Andrés! That would

have made most people run away. But you just love the pressure!'

After another Portugal miss, Spain were one kick away. Cesc stepped up and made no mistake. They had done it. 'Another final!' Andrés screamed as they sprinted to the corner flag to celebrate with Cesc and their goalkeeper, Iker Casillas. 'This is incredible!'

It was only a few hours later that it all began to sink in for Andrés. Without even thinking about it, he had volunteered to take a penalty in a European Championships semi-final.

'Winning on penalties is such a great feeling!' he said loudly once they were back in the dressing room. 'What a buzz!'

'Well, for some of us, it's not exactly great for the heart rate!' Vicente replied. José Antonio would later admit to Andrés that he was too nervous to watch the shootout, even before knowing that Andrés was taking one of the penalties.

Vicente had already hugged all the players out on the pitch and now he was going round the room dishing out more hugs. 'Andrés, you shocked me when you wanted to take a penalty. But what a beauty. You buried it!'

'Sergio, I'm surprised you didn't balloon yours over the bar!' Andrés called across the dressing room. Sergio had missed wildly in the Champions League semi-final shootout.

Sergio gave him a look as the rest of the players giggled.

'Too soon for that joke?' Andres asked, with a cheeky grin.

They both burst out laughing.

'I got it right today!' Sergio said. 'That's all that counts.'

The celebrations lasted another hour or two, then everyone grew serious again. They hadn't won the trophy yet.

'That was close!' Busqi told Andrés as they climbed wearily out of the bus. 'We've got to take our chances otherwise Italy could punish us.'

As Andrés glanced around the hotel meeting room on the morning of the final, he saw a determined, focused look on every face.

Vicente marched in, clapping his hands.

'This is it. Some of you won at Euro 2008, many of you won at the 2010 World Cup. This won't be any easier. No posing.'

'I think he's talking to you,' Xavi whispered to Sergio, sparking more laughter – Barcelona and Real Madrid giggling together despite the clubs' heated rivalry. Even Vicente joined in.

'That reminds me,' Vicente said. 'Remember what I told you before the tournament? No matter what is going on between Barcelona and Real Madrid, you leave that baggage at the door when you put on the Spain shirt. And that's exactly what you've done. I couldn't be prouder. Now go and make history.'

They all clapped. Andrés smiled. It was so true. Despite Barcelona's nasty battles against Real Madrid – against Sergio, against Iker – they had never lost sight of their respect and friendship.

In the final, Spain scored an early goal against Italy and never looked back, eventually coasting to a 4-0 victory with Andrés and Xavi at their best, sweeping the ball around midfield. 'It's hard to believe we couldn't score in 120 minutes in the semi-final,' he shouted to Xavi after they scored the fourth.

And so it was a familiar end to a major tournament for Spain – and for Andrés. Three major international trophies in a row. History-makers. They lifted the trophy, the music blasted in the dressing room and the champagne flowed. Andrés was named Man of the Match and Player of the Tournament. 'Show-off!' Gerard joked as Andrés walked in holding his trophies.

As Andrés had learned over the years, there was nothing better than sitting back with his teammates and enjoying the success.

'This is going to make me sound old,' he began, sitting next to Sergio, Xavi and Fernando that night for a beer and recapping their Euro 2012 run. 'But long after we've retired, people are still going to be talking about what we've achieved together. Euro 2008, the 2010 World Cup and Euro 2012. We've dominated Europe, we've dominated the world. This may never happen again.'

They all fell silent, deep in thought.

'So let's keep it going,' Sergio finally added. 'Why not win the World Cup again as well?'

They all smiled. 'I'll drink to that,' Fernando replied.

'Cheers!' they said together, clinking their glasses.

CHAPTER 18

CHASING MORE TROPHIES

Back at Barcelona, the trophies kept on coming. With Andrés, Xavi and Leo in top form, no one could stop them in La Liga. Pep had moved on, but new manager Tito Vilanova kept the momentum going. They clinched the 2012/13 title while losing only twice.

'What an achievement!' Andrés said, as he inspected his winner's medal. 'I can't believe we got 100 points.'

During a break back in Fuentealbilla over the summer, Andrés had a chance to catch up with his old friends Abelardo and Julian.

They had almost finished their lunch and Julian

was checking something on his phone. He suddenly looked up.

'Andrés, can you believe all the trophies you've won? I'm looking at the list: so far you've got six La Liga titles, three Champions League trophies, two Spanish Cups, five Spanish Super Cups, two UEFA Super Cups, two FIFA Club World Cups, two European Championships, one World Cup. Wow! How do you even have room for all those medals?!'

'It's a good job we taught him everything he knows,' Abelardo chimed in, grinning. 'And don't forget that he has been in the top three for the Ballon D'Or trophy. If you ask me, you should have won it one of those years.'

Andrés was feeling uncomfortable with all this talk of his success. 'I'm just doing my job. I've been lucky to play with some incredible players.'

But the challenge of maintaining such high standards was starting to have an impact, even if Andrés didn't realise it yet.

The 2013/14 season was not so easy, as Atletico Madrid rose up to win La Liga and Real Madrid lifted the Champions League trophy. 'It's tough to watch,' Andrés said to Anna as he watched those two teams face off in the Champions League final.

'You can't win it all every year,' Anna replied. 'Sometimes you need these little disappointments to get you fired up again.'

'Look at you, my little football expert! You've come a long way since the night we met at El Teatro!'

Anna giggled. 'I don't think "expert" is the right word. But I know more than I ever thought I would. And I love shocking my family with Barcelona facts!'

Still reeling from missing out on the big trophies that season, Andrés joined up with the rest of the Spain squad, ready for the 2014 World Cup in Brazil. They were one of the big talking points – everyone wanted to see if they could keep their major tournament run going.

Andrés felt good about their chances, even though they were in a tough group with the Netherlands, Chile and Australia. There was so much experience in the Spain squad.

'Look, we know the Netherlands are going to be

out for revenge,' Vicente cautioned his team before the first game. 'They have a point to prove. Keep your heads and move the ball.'

When Spain took the lead, all the signs were positive. But then it all fell apart. The defence, which had been so solid in previous tournaments, was all over the place as the Dutch stormed back to win 5-1.

Andrés could hardly believe it. Every time he urged his teammates to settle down and keep the ball for a few minutes, the opposition swarmed everywhere and broke up the Spanish attacks.

He trudged back to the dressing room, head down. What a disaster! He knew he could have played better but it had been a bad day for the whole team.

'Forget the score!' Vicente said. 'A loss is a loss. It's just the first game. If we beat Chile, we're right back in it.'

But even Andrés, who was usually so positive, now had a bad feeling about the tournament. That first performance had been so unlike them but he wasn't sure how to fix things.

Things got worse in the next game against Chile.

Andrés had lots of the ball but Spain as a team went nowhere. Chile won 2-0 and Spain were out.

'I can't believe it!' Andrés said quietly as he sat in the dressing room after the game. He felt sick. He couldn't even bring himself to get changed.

Anna did her best to comfort him when he called that night. 'I know this won't really help at the moment, but just try to remember all the amazing moments you've given the fans in the past few tournaments,' she said.

There was still time to restore some pride in the final group game against Australia. 'Let's prove that the first two games weren't the real Spain,' Andrés told his teammates as they prepared for the warm-up.

A 3-0 win over Australia made him feel a little better, but the disappointment of elimination was still fresh. He knew he hadn't been at his best and he couldn't remember the last time he had been knocked out of a tournament so early.

As he boarded the plane that would take the team home from Brazil, he promised himself that he would bounce back next season.

CHAPTER 19

BACK TO HIS BEST

Entering the 2014/15 season, Andrés was more motivated than ever. He was determined to bounce back from the previous season. His form had dipped and he had read a few newspaper articles suggesting that his best days were behind him.

'One season where I'm not quite at my best and people think I'm finished?' he said to Anna as the season began. 'I guess that's the football world.'

Anna smiled. 'I get the feeling that these so-called experts will regret their words. You've got that look in your eye.'

'We need a big year. Last season was a

disappointment and the World Cup was a nightmare.
It's time to put that right. We can do it.'

'You can do it, Daddy!' Valeria suddenly said.

Andrés and Anna laughed. Valeria was too young to
understand the conversation but she liked to join in.

'Well now I definitely know we can do it,' Andrés
said, kissing his daughter's cheek.

The Barcelona midfield was changing. With
Xavi entering his final season, new manager Luis
Enrique began looking to the future and made the
trio of Andrés, Ivan and Busqi his preferred choice.
With Xavi playing fewer minutes, Andrés was the
replacement captain.

Barcelona stormed through the season, with Andrés
leading the charge. He had another Treble in his
sights. Real Madrid pushed them all the way in La
Liga but Barcelona held on for yet another title. A
3-1 victory in the Spanish Cup final meant that, just
like in 2011, Andrés and his teammates only needed
the Champions League trophy to complete their set.
Vowing to stop them in that final were Juventus.

'We have to watch out for Andrea Pirlo,' Luis

Enrique lectured his players before the game. 'If we don't, he can control the midfield.'

Andrés took that as a challenge. It was *his* job to control midfield.

He had waited four years to be back in the Champions League final – and it took him not even five minutes to make his mark.

'Play me in,' he screamed.

Before the ball reached him, he already knew what he wanted to do. He used a quick dribble to pull defenders towards him, then laid the ball off for Ivan Rakitić to score from close range.

'That was beautiful,' Dani Alves yelled, hugging Andrés and then jumping on Ivan's back. 'What a move.'

Barcelona kept Pirlo out of the game. Instead, it was Andrés running the show. He was everywhere. Picking up the ball deep and spraying passes to the wings, then roaming forward to set up chances.

Just like in 2011, Barcelona were pegged back, despite playing well. In the second half Juventus scored and suddenly their momentum returned.

But Andrés didn't panic. He just settled everyone down with his passing. When Leo's shot bounced loose, Luis Suárez was there to put Barcelona back in front. He hurdled the advertising boards as part of the goal celebration and Andrés chased after him. When Neymar added a third moments later, Andrés knew it was all over. He was going to be a Champions League winner again!

'We were overdue,' he said to Gerard Piqué after they shook hands with the Juventus players. 'The four-year drought is over. We're champions of Europe again!'

Andrés was named Man of the Match, just adding to his big game reputation. 'We just don't lose finals!' he said to Dani. He didn't care if it sounded a bit cocky. 'Somehow, we always find a way.'

As Andrés and his teammates waited for Xavi to lead them up the steps to lift the trophy, Andrés felt a tap on his back. He turned to see Xavi, who was leaving the team after seventeen years. 'Lead the way, maestro,' he said, pointing for Andrés to walk up with him.

'No, this is your moment. You deserve to have it all to yourself.'

'We've done everything together, Andrés. This is the way I want it. I want to share this with you.'

Andrés could tell Xavi would not be persuaded. He hugged him. 'This is so special. What are we going to do without you?'

'You'll be just fine. The club is in good hands, Andrés. *Your* hands.'

CHAPTER 20

LEADING FROM THE FRONT

Just before Andrés headed off for a summer break, he dropped into the Nou Camp to clear out his locker and say goodbye to the staff. Luis Enrique heard Andrés speaking with one of the coaches and poked his head out of his office.

'Andrés, can you drop by once you're done?' he said.

'Sure, boss.'

Andrés was curious. He quickly packed up his things and returned to see his manager.

'Hi, Andrés. I won't keep you long, but I wanted to discuss one thing ahead of next season.'

'You're planning for that already?'

'Well, just a few details,' Luis Enrique said. 'What else am I supposed to do all summer?'

They both laughed.

'Andrés, you've been a huge part of what this club has achieved over the past ten years. And you've been at Barcelona since you were, what, twelve?'

Andrés nodded.

'You have such an influence in the dressing room. The older players and the younger players all look up to you, and you've never put a foot wrong here, on or off the pitch.'

'Well, I did miss that one sitter last season!' Andrés joked.

'How could I forget! But, seriously, what I'm building up to is this: we want you to be the new Barcelona club captain.'

A huge smile broke out across Andrés's face.

'I'd be honoured!'

'I know you wore the armband a lot last season when Xavi wasn't playing, but this will be different. You're the guy now. This is your show.'

'I can't wait for the challenge, boss. This club means everything to me.'

As he sat in his car in the stadium car park, Andrés began to share the news. He called Anna and heard her scream with joy. 'Andrés, that's amazing news.'

That reaction was only topped by his parents. Andrés could only hear every fifth word as they sobbed on the phone.

That night, he felt like he was walking on air.

'Things around here are going to be crazy,' Anna said, rubbing her stomach. Their second child was due any day now. 'In a good way, of course, but with the baby and the captaincy, you'll need to find some magic way to stay fresh.'

He gave her a sleepy smile. 'I'm tired just thinking about it, but we'll make it work!'

Before he knew it, he was back at the training ground, preparing for the new season and doing his part for all the club's promotions. The fixture list was out and he had already circled some of the big games.

It all started with the home friendly against Roma – his first home game as club captain.

'Come on, get going!' Anna said. 'You should get there early to really make the most of the moment. You have to set a good example!'

Andrés smiled. 'Okay, okay. I'll see you all later!' He kissed Anna and then his little son, Paolo Andrea, who was fast asleep in her arms.

He turned the music up in the car and tapped the steering wheel to the beat.

At the Nou Camp, people were smiling at him and shaking his hand everywhere he went. 'Go and take care of business,' Luis Enrique said as they hugged outside the dressing room.

Before long, everyone had got changed and were just sitting in the dressing room, waiting to walk out to the tunnel. 'Andrés, where's the armband?' Gerard called.

Andrés smiled. 'I'm saving it until the last minute – just to build more excitement.'

'Seriously? You score that goal against Chelsea and the winner in the World Cup final and you still need more excitement in your life?!'

Andrés had worried over the summer that being captain – and the extra responsibilities that it brought

– might have an impact on his form. But he was relieved to see that he was playing as well as ever.

In November 2015, as he led Barcelona out against Real Madrid at the Bernabéu Stadium, he just knew he was going to have a big game.

He got on the ball early, working it into the gaps and controlling the pace. The Real midfielders couldn't get near him. Barcelona raced into an early lead, then Andrés helped to double it. Again, he found himself in space and dribbled towards goal. At the perfect moment, he laid the ball through to Neymar, whose shot sneaked past the goalkeeper and into the net.

'Great pass, captain,' Neymar shouted, hugging Andrés.

Andrés wasn't finished yet. Again, Real Madrid made the mistake of not closing him down. He darted forward and played the ball to Neymar on the edge of the box. 'One-two,' he yelled as he continued his run. Neymar gave him a clever back heel and Andrés smashed an unstoppable shot into the top corner.

Goooooooooooooooooaaaaaaaaaaaaaaaaaalllllllllllllll lllllllllll!!!!!!

The Barcelona coaches and substitutes were up off the bench cheering. Andrés charged off to celebrate, with his teammates sprinting after him.

'Listen to the Real Madrid fans,' Busqi called to him. 'They're screaming and booing, and we're just making it worse with every goal.'

As the minutes ticked down, the referee blew his whistle to stop the game for a substitution. Andrés saw his number go up on the board. His first reaction was disappointment – they were running riot and he wanted to stay on until the end. The crowd was still booing loudly.

Then something changed. As he jogged towards the touchline, the boos turned to cheers. Andrés didn't understand at first. He looked around, then realised they were clapping for him. A Barcelona player getting a standing ovation at the Bernabéu was a rare moment, but Andrés had been incredible that night. He raised his hand to acknowledge the cheers and then sat down behind Luis Enrique.

'Pretty special, huh?' his manager said, turning round.

Andrés smiled and nodded. It really was.

He rarely stopped to celebrate these moments for long but, every now and again, he allowed himself a minute to think about everything he had won with Barcelona and Spain. World champion and European champion with club and country – the boy from Fuentealbilla had done it all!

But there was always another trophy to chase and he was happy to be leading the way. When his parents came to visit during the season, they loved to talk about his career and everything he had achieved. 'Andrés, when you look back at the last ten years, you must be so proud,' his mum Mari said one afternoon as they all sat at the dinner table.

'I am,' Andrés replied. 'It has been an incredible journey, but I still believe that...'

He looked at Anna with a big smile and together they said their favourite phrase.

'...the best is yet to come!'

Turn the page for a sneak preview of
another brilliant football story by
Matt and Tom Oldfield. . .

LUIS SUAREZ

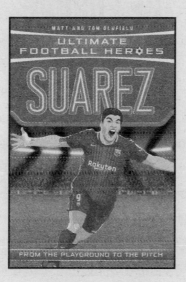

Available now!

CHAPTER 1

CHAMPION
OF EUROPE

6 June 2015. As Luis took a quick glance around the stadium, all he saw were the colours of Barcelona. It was still thirty minutes before kick-off but they were cheering as if the warm-up was the real thing. He stretched out his right leg, loosening the muscles and preparing his body for the biggest game of his life.

Xavi fired the ball towards him, catching him by surprise, and Luis turned to chase it as it rolled off the pitch. As he crossed the touchline, almost within touching distance of the Barcelona fans in the front row, all he heard was 'Suárez! Suárez!' He grinned and gave the fans a quick wave. They were ready for this Champions League Final – and so was he.

Hard times make you appreciate the good times – that had been Luis's motto over the past year. After all the anger, the tears, the headlines and the four-month suspension, he had bounced back better than ever. There was nothing he could do about his mistakes in the past, except try to learn from them. He had shut out all the distractions and focused on only two things: football and family. Now, having already won the Spanish league title and the Spanish Cup, he was ninety minutes away from completing an amazing Treble.

Back in the dressing room, Dani Alves turned the music up loud and the players tried their best to relax. Luis walked over to the far side, where the 'Suárez 9' shirt was hanging. He had worn that name and number plenty of times but it had never looked better than it did now. He looked up at the countdown timer high on the wall – less than fifteen minutes to go. He put on the shirt, pulled up his socks and slotted in a tiny pair of shin pads. Their opponents, Juventus, would play a physical style, but Luis had never liked big, bulky shin pads. He could handle the kicks.

'Dani, throw me the tape,' he called.

'Do I work for you now?' Dani replied, laughing.
'Just because you score the goals, you think you run
the place?'

Luis had quickly built good friendships within
the Barcelona squad. For the first time since leaving
Uruguay, he was surrounded by teammates who
spoke Spanish, and that had certainly helped him
to settle in quickly. He still had to pinch himself to
believe that he was scoring goals alongside a magician
like Lionel Messi.

The referee knocked on the dressing-room door.
It was time. Luis finished putting the tape round his
wrist, jumped to his feet and joined in the quick high
fives. As they headed for the tunnel, he felt a hand
on his shoulder and turned to see Xavi waiting with
some final words of advice. 'Stay calm out there.
They know all about your temper and they'll be
trying to wind you up. Play your game and ignore
them. We need you.'

Luis nodded. Many of the things he regretted most
in his football career were related to reckless moments

on the pitch. He just needed to win every game, and sometimes he went too far. 'Don't worry. I won't let you guys down,' he added with a serious face. Then a grin broke out. 'After the game, it'll just be my goals that people are talking about.'

For most of his teammates, this was yet another Champions League Final. But it was Luis's first and he was shaking with a combination of nerves and excitement. The atmosphere was incredible – the anthem, the fans, the perfect pitch. It was like no other game he had ever played.

As he passed the ball around in a little triangle with Messi and Neymar, he had no doubts about the result of the game. With all their star players, how could they not score three or four goals? He placed the ball in the centre circle. He would be getting the first touch of the final! When the whistle blew for kick-off, Luis felt like he could run all day.

Barcelona took an early lead and Juventus equalised in the second half, but Luis struggled to find his best form. Was it just the big occasion that was getting to him? He worked hard but nothing was falling for him.

With twenty-five minutes to go, he even feared that he might be substituted. Clapping his hands, he urged his teammates to do more, saying, 'Leo, let's go. Let's make something happen.'

One of Luis's biggest strengths was that he never gave up and always believed that a chance would come his way. From his earliest years, he just knew where to be at the right moment to score goals. There's still time, he told himself. Things can change in a second.

Then it happened. Messi dribbled past three Juventus defenders, and Luis saw his teammate preparing to take a shot. His instincts took over. He wasn't going to watch the shot. As soon as Messi pulled his leg back to shoot, Luis was racing towards the goal, looking for a rebound. Juventus goalkeeper Gianluigi Buffon made the save but the ball bounced loose. None of the defenders had a chance. Luis was too quick. Before they could move, he had pounced on the ball and fired a shot into the top corner.

Suddenly, as the emotions took over, everything was a blur. He jumped over the advertising boards

onto the athletics track that surrounded the pitch.
Lionel, Neymar, Dani and the rest of his teammates
joined him, climbing on his back and burying him in
hugs. He had saved the day. 'That was such a classic
Suárez goal,' Dani yelled. 'You shoot, you score –
that's why you're El Pistolero!'

As he jogged back to the halfway line, Luis couldn't
stop smiling. He loved scoring in big finals. From the
first time he kicked a ball, he had always wanted
to be the goalscorer and the hero. While the game
was stopped for a substitution, he allowed his mind
to wander, just for a minute, back to his beloved
Uruguay, where it all began.

ANDRÉS INIESTA HONOURS

Barcelona

🏆 La Liga: 2004–05, 2005–06, 2008–09, 2009–10, 2010–11, 2012–13, 2014–15, 2015–16

🏆 Copa del Rey: 2008–09, 2011–12, 2014–15, 2015–16

🏆 UEFA Champions League: 2005–06, 2008–09, 2010–11, 2014–15

Spain

🏆 FIFA World Cup: 2010

🏆 UEFA European Championship: 2008, 2012

🏆 UEFA European Under-19 Championship: 2002

🏆 UEFA European Under-17 Championship: 2001

Individual

🏆 La Liga Spanish Player of the Year: 2009

🏆 FIFA Ballon d'Or, runner-up: 2010

🏆 FIFA World Cup Final Man of the Match: 2010

🏆 FIFA World Cup Dream Team: 2010

🏆 UEFA Best Player in Europe Award: 2012

🏆 FIFA Ballon d'Or, third place: 2012

🏆 UEFA European Championship Final Man of the Match: 2012

🏆 UEFA Euro Player of the Tournament: 2012

🏆 UEFA Champions League Team of the Season: 2014–15, 2015–16

🏆 UEFA Champions League Final Man of the Match: 2015

INIESTA

8 THE FACTS

NAME:
Andrés Iniesta Luján

DATE OF BIRTH:
11 May 1984

AGE: 33

PLACE OF BIRTH:
Fuentealbilla

NATIONALITY: Spain

BEST FRIEND: Abelardo

CURRENT CLUB: Barcelona

POSITION: CM

THE STATS

Height (cm):	**171**
Club appearances:	**684**
Club goals:	**60**
Club trophies:	**30**
International appearances:	**117**
International goals:	**12**
International trophies:	**3**
Ballon d'Ors:	**0**

★ ★ ★ **HERO RATING: 89** ★ ★ ★

GREATEST MOMENTS

Type and search the web links to see the magic for yourself!

17 MAY 2006, BARCELONA 2-1 ARSENAL

https://www.youtube.com/watch?v=VsdMmDwCY10

2005-2006 was a breakthrough season for Andrés. Just after his twenty-second birthday, he was named as a substitute for the Champions League final. When he came on at half-time, Arsenal were winning 1-0 but Andrés turned things around for Barcelona. His amazing pass set up the equaliser and soon, he was lifting his first Champions League trophy.

★2 6 MAY 2009, CHELSEA 1-1 BARCELONA

https://www.youtube.com/watch?v=1IrbMMzGMWA
With seconds to go in the Champions League semi-
final, Barcelona were heading out. They desperately
needed an away goal and Andrés was the man to score
it. The ball came to him on the edge of the penalty
area and he struck it powerfully and accurately into the
top corner. Andrés and his teammates went on to beat
Manchester United in the final.

★3 11 JULY 2010, NETHERLANDS 0-1 SPAIN (A.E.T.)

https://www.youtube.com/watch?v=QwADqit3dBE
At the 2010 World Cup in South Africa, Andrés was on
fire. He scored the winner against Chile in the group
stage but his best moment came in the 116th minute
of the final against the Netherlands. Andrés started
the move with a clever backheel and finished it with a
brilliant left-foot finish. In that instant, he became Spain's
national hero.

1 JULY 2012, SPAIN 4-0 ITALY

https://www.youtube.com/watch?v=-oqZU1ll0eo
Andrés has always saved his best performances for the biggest games. He didn't score in the Euro 2012 final but he was Man of the Match and Player of the Tournament. In central midfield, he dominated the game with his quick passes and clever running. The Italians had no chance of stopping him.

21 NOVEMBER 2015, REAL MADRID 0-4 BARCELONA

https://www.youtube.com/watch?v=DhFBGYNm4qI
Not many Barcelona players have been clapped by the Real Madrid fans but they clapped Andrés after this man of the match performance away at the Bernabeu. Wearing the captain's armband, he set up one goal for Neymar and then scored a great goal of his own. Andrés showed that he was still one of the world's top superstars.

PLAY LIKE YOUR HEROES

ANDRÉS INIESTA'S
LA CROQUETA

SEE IT HERE You Tube

https://www.youtube.com/watch?v=UkyeZDMpclk

STEP 1: Get the ball in a busy area and wait for a midfielder to dive in for the tackle.

STEP 2: At the last second, drag the ball away by moving it from your right foot to your left foot.

STEP 3: Quickly move the ball back from your left foot to your right foot, like you're playing a one-two with yourself. Close control is essential here.

STEP 4: Dribble past the midfielder, who is probably now lying on the grass.

STEP 5: If you're feeling confident, repeat the trick on the next midfielder.

STEP 6: If not, look up and play a defence-splitting pass for your striker to score.

TEST YOUR KNOWLEDGE

QUESTIONS

1. What was the name of Andrés' first football club?

2. How old was Andrés when he moved to Barcelona's *La Masia* academy?

3. Who were the first two friends that Andrés made at *La Masia*?

4. Who did Andrés' Barcelona play against in the final of the 1999 Nike Cup and what was the score?

5. Which Barcelona manager gave Andrés his first-team debut and how old was he?

6. Which of Andrés' childhood heroes went on to become his manager at Barcelona?

7. Andrés was in the Barcelona starting line-up for the 2006 Champions League final – true or false?

8. What was the first big international tournament that Andrés went to with Spain?

9. Andrés was in the Barcelona starting line-up for the 2009 Champions League final – true or false?

10. How many times has Andrés finished in the Top 3 for the Ballon d'Or award?

11. Who did Andrés replace as Barcelona captain in 2015?

Answers below. . . No cheating!

1. *Albacete.* 2. *Twelve.* 3. *Jorge and Victor Valdés.* 4. *Barcelona faced Argentinian team Rosario in the final and they won 2-1 thanks to Andrés' last-minute winner.* 5. *Louis van Gaal was the manager and Andrés was only 18 when he played against Bruges in the Champions League.* 6. *Pep Guardiola.* 7. *False – he came on at half-time against Arsenal and changed the game.* 8. *The 2006 World Cup in Germany.* 9. *True – despite lots of injuries during the season, Andrés played for 92 minutes as Barcelona beat Manchester United.* 10. *2 – he came 2nd in 2010 and 3rd in 2012. Lionel Messi won both times.* 11. *Xavi.*

HAVE YOU GOT THEM ALL?

ULTIMATE FOOTBALL HEROES